# The Library of Author Biographies

# Lois Lowry

The Library of Author Biographies

# LOIS LOWRY

New Lenox
Public Library District
120 Veterans Parkway
New Lenox, Illinois 60451

## Susanna Daniel

Published in 2003 by The Rosen Publishing Group, Inc.
29 East 21st Street, New York, NY 10010

First Edition       **3 1984 00210 0566**

**Library of Congress Cataloging-in-Publication Data**

Daniel, Susanna.
Lois Lowry / Susanna Daniel.
   p. cm. — (The library of author biographies)
Includes bibliographical references and index.
ISBN 0-8239-3775-5 (lib. bdg.)
1. Lowry, Lois—Juvenile literature. 2. Authors, American—20th century—Biography—Juvenile literature. 3. Children's stories—Authorship—Juvenile literature. I. Title. II. Series.
PS3562.O923 Z645 2003
813'.54—dc21

                                        200200745208249-3775-5

*Manufactured in the United States of America*

# Table of Contents

# Introduction: On Top of the World

In 1993, when Lois Lowry won her second Newbery Medal—the highest honor awarded to books written for children—she was traveling on a ship in Antarctica. Her publisher, unable to reach her by phone, sent a telegram to the ship. Lois was very excited when she read the telegram, but because she prefers to travel alone, there was no one with whom to share the good news. She turned to a stranger who was standing nearby. "You've probably never heard of this," she said to the woman, "but I just won the Newbery Medal."

"My goodness," said the woman. "I'm the former president of the American Library

Association." As it turned out, the woman was indeed very familiar with the Newbery Award. When Lowry accepted the award, she said that upon receiving the news, she felt like she was "at the top of the world at the bottom of the world."[1]

Incidentally, when the telephone rang four years earlier, and she learned that she had won the first of her two Newbery Awards, for her novel *Number the Stars* (1989), she was busy doing something that she does for hours every day, something she's done almost every day for more than twenty years: She was sitting at her desk, writing.

All those hours have paid off: Lowry has written more than twenty-five books to date. Her first book, *A Summer to Die*, was published in 1977, and during the 1980s she became well-known for her series of books about a lively and rebellious adolescent girl named Anastasia Krupnik. By the 1990s, Lowry had become one of the most popular and highly respected authors writing for young adolescents. And she's still writing.

Like many authors, most of Lowry's books deal with a few broad themes. Some of the themes that reappear in her books are human connections and relationships, saying good-bye, and fitting in. For example, *Find a Stranger, Say Goodbye* (1978) is about a seventeen-year-old girl who meets her birth mother after living her entire life with the family that adopted her, and *Number the Stars* is about a girl living in Denmark in 1943, during the time when Nazi soldiers were "relocating" Jewish citizens. *A Summer to Die* is about a girl whose sister is dying of cancer.

Generally speaking, Lowry writes three kinds of novels: 1) funny, lighthearted books, such as the Anastasia Krupnik series; 2) realistic and serious books about difficult situations, such as *Find a Stranger, Say Goodbye* and *Number the Stars*; and 3) futuristic novels set in imaginary settings, such as *The Giver* (1993).

As far back as she can remember, Lowry wanted to be a novelist. When she accepted her first Newbery Medal in 1990, Lowry said in her speech that for years she'd carried in her wallet two fortunes from Chinese fortune cookies. "I saved these two because I have wanted each of them to come true," she said. "One says: 'YOU WILL BE FAMOUS IN A FAR-OUT PROFESSION.' And the other: 'YOU WILL ATTEND A PARTY WHERE STRANGE CUSTOMS PREVAIL.'"[2]

Is writing a far-out profession? Maybe it's not for some people, but for Lowry it was, at least in the beginning, because she was a mother with four young children and her husband, Donald Grey Lowry, was a full-time lawyer. She recalls getting up from her desk to cook a meal or pick up one of her children from school or sports practice. "There were a number of years when there was a well-worn path between the typewriter and the washing machine," says Lowry about this period of her life. "The first money I ever earned went to hire a housekeeper, and whenever I am asked if there was any one person who influenced my career, I make a short speech of tribute to a Czechoslovakian woman named Marga, who for years dealt with my children's lost sneakers and vacuumed around a soporific [sleepy] Newfoundland dog."[3]

As for the prediction that Lowry would attend a party with strange customs, she said in her speech, "This is certainly a very fine party. Is it a strange custom, the awarding of the Newbery Medal?" Later, she answered her own question: "It is not a strange custom, after all, to remind the world that there is an unending value to the work we all do on behalf of children."[4]

Lowry has said that she thinks the Newbery Award should be awarded to an author only once. As she said in an interview, "It didn't seem fair that one person should receive it twice. It was my editor who pointed out to me that the medal is given to a book, not a person. I like keeping that in mind."[5] (For a list of selected awards Lowry has won, see the back of this book.)

Lowry has a talent for turning ordinary life into good reading. Her characters are lively and sometimes unusual, but they are basically regular kids. Her popular Anastasia Krupnik series, for example, follows a family—Anastasia Krupnik, her parents, and her little brother, Sam—as they work as a team to overcome life's little challenges. In one book, Anastasia decides that she hates her own name. In another, she must cope with her family's move to the suburbs. The main concern that plagues Anastasia throughout her books, the source of all of her problems, is one to which almost any adolescent can relate: She is afraid that she is strange.

In one of hundreds of rave reviews of the Anastasia Krupnik books, Joseph B. Browne wrote, "Anastasia Krupnik is a typical child of today! She has her own ideas . . . nor is she likely to change her views easily. This, though, is what gives her such an appealing personality . . . Loaded within the pages are bits of dialogue, situation, and character certain to bring chuckles, smiles, and perhaps even a bit of insight into the personal lives of girls grades three through six."[6]

Anastasia was modeled on Amy Carter, the daughter of Jimmy Carter, who was president in the late 1970s. According to Lowry, "Because [Amy Carter] was the President's daughter, she was in the news a lot, and I always got a kick out of seeing her because she misbehaved, often in public, and I always cringed, thinking, 'What would I do if I were the President and my daughter acted like that?' But also, she seemed very real, a normal kid, and so for the first book about Anastasia, which described that child, I had Amy Carter in mind. Even her appearance. I described Anastasia as a kind of scrawny, ten-year-old kid with glasses and scraggly blonde hair."[7]

Lowry's memories of her own childhood, in addition to her experiences as a mother, directly influence her work. "Until I was about twelve," Lowry confessed in an interview, "I thought my parents were terrific, wise, and wonderful, beautiful, loving, and well-dressed. By age twelve and a half, they turned into stupid, boring people with whom I did not want to be seen in public." She continued, "That happens to all kids, and to the kids in my books as well."[8]

Anastasia, for example, is baffled by her parents' odd habits—like her father keeping his poetry manuscripts in the freezer—as well as by her own limitations, like her inability to climb a rope in gym class. In 1988, Lowry started writing books about Anastasia's younger brother, Sam. To date, there are eleven books about Anastasia and Sam, and Lowry has said repeatedly that she is still very fond of the whole Krupnik family, and she has no plans to stop writing about them.

Although the Krupnik books are lighthearted in tone, many of Lowry's other books are more serious. Many of her books deal with difficult subjects, such as death and abandonment. Lowry believes that kids growing up today are too mature to be convinced by picture-perfect ideas of the world, and she believes that readers can learn from characters with whom they identify. When she was a child, many popular books—including J. D. Salinger's *Catcher in the Rye* (1951)—were off-limits to young readers because of the harsh realities they portrayed. (Today, *Catcher in the Rye* is as popular as ever, though it still tops the list of books most often banned or challenged by libraries and schools.)

One of Lowry's strengths as an author is her ability to create characters who have the intelligence and wisdom to overcome life's obstacles, both large and small. In the Krupnik books, Anastasia and Sam face minor, day-to-day challenges, and in Lowry's more serious books, the characters confront more intimidating problems. No one has ever said life was easy—not in the real world, and not in Lois Lowry's fiction. But Lowry's characters never shrink in the face of trouble—more often than not, they look to friends and relatives for guidance, and ultimately they triumph.

# 1 Writing

Lois Lowry, originally named Lois Ann Hammersburg, was born on March 20, 1937, in Honolulu, Hawaii, where her father, who was a dentist in the military, was stationed. Her mother was a schoolteacher and homemaker. Lois had started reading and writing by the time she was three years old. Lowry recalled a letter sent home by her nursery school teacher, declaring that "her unusual ability to read and write sets her apart from the other children."[1]

Writing and reading were always Lowry's number-one passions. In an autobiographical essay written for the *Something About the Author Series* (SAAS), Lowry said that she was aware, early on, that she was different from

14

other kids, and that she disliked the games they played, so she spent most of her time sitting alone in a corner of the classroom, reading. "An intellectual snob at the age of three,"[2] she wrote in the essay. She was such an advanced reader that she skipped the second grade altogether.

Lowry started writing books when she was just a child, but rarely finished any of them. "It's very easy to start a book, whether you're ten or sixty," she told students. "It's much harder to finish one."[3] As an adolescent, she liked the public library more than she liked school. She often visited the library twice in one day, until the librarian told her that she was not supposed to return books the same day she checked them out. After that, Lois started taking home only the thickest books, which promised to last longer than one afternoon.

Lowry's family moved to Brooklyn, New York, in 1939, and her father went to World War II in 1942. During the war, with her father stationed overseas, her family lived with her mother's parents in Carlisle, Pennsylvania. After the war ended, Lois's family moved to Tokyo, Japan, to join her father. They lived in Japan through Lowry's junior high years. Eventually, Lowry learned to speak Japanese fluently, though as an adult she remembers only a few phrases.

Lowry was eight years old when World War II ended. About the impact of living in post-war Japan as a child, Lowry says, "Just as I came into awareness, it was a world that included both the atomic bombs, and the destruction in Hiroshima and Nagasaki, and the newsreels of the horror of what was going on in Germany: the death camps and the tragedies there. These were the images of my early adolescence."[4] (Hiroshima and Nagasaki are cities in Japan that were devastated by atomic bombs during World War II. The Holocaust in Germany occurred at the same time.)

"My childhood in Japan influenced me, of course, even though I haven't specifically set fiction there. Those years [ages eleven through thirteen] are crucial to a child's development. That I happened to spend them in Japan probably simply added an awareness at that age of cultural differences, of feelings of alienation, and an appreciation of the richness of history and geography that I would not have had so young if I had stayed in [America]. Everything a writer experiences as a young person goes into the later writing in some form."[5]

Lowry's mother brought the children back to live in Pennsylvania in 1950, but her father stayed behind in Japan. The next year, the family moved to Governor's Island in New York City.

Lowry figured out early on that she was not a gifted athlete. She doesn't regret this, but rather she appreciates the skills that came to her naturally, including her excellent handwriting and her way with words. In high school, she worked on a literary magazine, but she never enjoyed group activities. She mostly preferred—then and now—solitary activities, like movies and gardening and, of course, writing. By the time she graduated high school, at age sixteen, she knew she wanted to be a novelist. During adolescence, Lowry was an introvert and a daydreamer, as well as an enthusiastic reader, unlike Anastasia, who is very outgoing. "In a way," says Lowry, "Anastasia is the child I always yearned to be. Perhaps that's why I created her."[6]

Lowry considers herself fortunate to have been born the middle child of three children. Her older sister, Helen, like their mother, was soft-spoken, pleasant, and gentle. Her younger brother, Jon, the only boy, shared their father's interest in electric trains and, in adulthood, car mechanics. Because of the family dynamics, Lowry spent a lot of time on her own.

Lowry says she was "a solitary child who lived in the world of books and [her] own imagination."[7] Though she doesn't wish loneliness on her readers, she hopes her books can help readers feel less alone the way the books she read as a child—which ranged from Bobbsey Twin mysteries to Betty Smith's classic, *A Tree Grows in Brooklyn* (1943)—helped her. In her autobiography, *Looking Back: A Book of Memories* (1998), Lowry wrote about having read *The Yearling* (1938) as a child; *The Yearling* is about a boy who befriends a deer, only to have to end the deer's life at the end of the book. "My mother read *The Yearling* to [my sister] Helen and me." Lowry continued, "I was nine; Helen was twelve. Mother sat in the hall outside our bedrooms and read aloud. I thought *The Yearling* was the most wonderful book I'd ever encountered. It made me want to be a boy. It made me want to be poor and live in a swamp, where I would have animals as friends."[8]

Lowry also remembers reading a book by Lois Lenski called *Indian Captive: The Story of Mary Jemison* (1942). *Indian Captive* is based on the true story of a girl who is abducted from her home on the American frontier by Seneca Indians. Lenski, who lived from 1893 to 1974, wrote more than 100 books for children. In a speech Lowry gave at UCLA in 1997, she said, "I knew that [Mary's] story was a true one, and that she had been brave when she was in danger. I knew that I could be, too. I think of the children who read my books. I wonder what armor they will need, what weaponry for their lives in these troubled times."[9]

In high school, a prediction printed with Lowry's photo in her yearbook read: "Future novelist." She attended Brown University in Rhode Island from 1954 to 1956, then left school at age nineteen to marry Donald Lowry. She worked part-time to help support her husband while he attended law school at Harvard University in Cambridge, Massachusetts.

She gave birth to their daughter Alix in 1958, then their son Grey was born the following year. Then came Kristin in 1961 and Benjamin in 1962. The family moved to Maine in 1963, and in 1972, Lowry earned her bachelor's degree in writing from the University of Southern Maine, which is located in Portland. Five years later, she and her husband divorced and Lowry published her first novel, *A Summer to Die*.

"In 1963, I was twenty-six years old," wrote Lowry in her SAAS essay. Of this time, Lowry says, "I had four children under the age of five. Come to think of it, so did my husband; but he also, by then, had a law degree from Harvard, so I think he got a little better end of the bargain than I did. I don't blame him, or anyone, for that. I blame the mindless culture of the [1950s], which did a lot of damage to decent people's lives."[10]

These days, Lowry lives in West Cambridge, Massachusetts, and spends weekends in New Hampshire. Her favorite food is Mexican, and she loves to travel. She knits, cooks, plays card games—especially bridge—and works in her garden. She loves to go to movies and she's always reading. Her books are organized on their shelves according to her own system. "I live a pretty quiet life,"[11] says Lowry.

For many years, Lowry has pursued photography in her spare time. In fact, she took the photographs that decorate the covers of *Number the Stars* and *The Giver*, in the paperback and hardcover editions. In an interview, Lowry said, "I have worked as a photographer and I love doing that, but unfortunately, I don't have time. For photographers, darkroom work is very time-consuming—I miss that, but I probably won't do it again."[12]

Walter Lorraine, Lowry's friend and editor at Houghton Mifflin, wrote about her generous spirit in an article for *Horn Book Magazine*. "Lois is a naturally forgiving person. I have never known her to be judgmental in any of our dealings. She accepts all people and attitudes as being necessary to life, and harbors no deep or hidden prejudices. I have never heard her badmouth a person. Whatever someone's action, or problems, she remains open and responsive. She sees reason and good in most human activity. For her, the glass is always half full. She listens, not superficially, as most of us do, but with attention. She makes you feel important, that she is involved and not merely a casual bystander. She truly hears what you have to say. Whatever the gripe or sad story, whether from a privileged ten-year-old or a poor aging vagrant, Lois listens."[13]

In an autobiographical sketch from 1983, Lowry described some of the treasures that clutter her Boston home. In addition to many, many books, Lowry's keepsakes include: all the records ever recorded by Billie Holiday, the great jazz vocalist from the 1930s and 1940s; a piece of tumbleweed from Idaho, sent by one of her fans (tumbleweed is a plant that breaks away from its roots and rolls around in the wind, hence the name); a hat decorated with the titles of all her books, sent by a seventh-grade class in Boylston, Massachusetts; and a patchwork quilt made by her great-great-grandmother.

# 2 How Lois Lowry Writes

O n June 26, 1994, months after she learned in Antarctica that she'd won her second Newbery Medal for her novel *The Giver* (1993), Lowry gave an acceptance speech in front of hundreds of members of the American Library Association in Miami, Florida. In her speech, Lowry said that she is often asked by aspiring young writers how she knows where to start. "I tell them that I just start where it feels right,"[1] she said.

Lowry has said that all her characters take shape in her imagination—even Anastasia Krupnik, who was originally modeled on Amy Carter, but who grew into a unique character. "But of course," she said, "my consciousness is filled with every child I've ever known, including my two grandchildren, my own kids (I had four) and especially myself as a child, because that person still lives inside me, too."[2]

Lowry writes every day. She starts at eight in the morning, in an office in her home, and continues through the afternoon. Sometimes she continues to work until three or four o'clock, with only a break for lunch. Says Lowry, "I go to work every day, the way real people go to work."[3]

It takes her about six months to write a book, plus some time for rewriting. After she's finished with each book, it spends about nine months in production with the publisher before it is printed and shipped to stores and libraries. In a recent interview with students, Lowry said, "I'm not a very well-organized writer. Beginnings come easily to me, but from there I usually start writing without a clear-cut idea of where I'm going." She does not, however, recommend this method for budding writers. Many writers, she pointed out, use outlines or index cards to map out a story before they begin writing. But not Lowry. She continued, "A lot of the fun and excitement of writing, for me, is because of the surprise of it: Each day in the creation of a book is a new adventure for me, and that wouldn't be true if I had a set of index cards telling me what was supposed to happen next."[4]

As for what to write about, Lowry claims that she never runs short on ideas. She is most interested in human connections of all kinds, including family relationships and friendships. "These are the things young people should pay attention to in their own lives," she said.[5]

Now that she has kids who have kids, Lowry understands better than ever how her family inspires her writing. As she put it, "I have grandchildren now. For them, I feel a greater urgency to do what I can do to convey the knowledge that we live intertwined on this planet and that our future as human beings depends on our caring more, and doing more, for one another." Through her relationships with her young grandchildren, Lowry can better understand how kids today think and behave, as well as what challenges and worries are most common. She continued, "The hard part is choosing which idea to focus on."[6]

When Lowry sits down to write a novel, in her mind she has imagined the main characters, the beginnings of the plot, and a sense of the theme. "The secondary characters and the complications of the plot all come to me after I begin writing, then I follow my imagination through the pages of the book. Parts of it take me by surprise when I'm writing. I have occasionally set a half-finished manuscript aside for a while and gone on to something different. But I always come back and finish what I've started. Right now I have several half-written books in my computer. Sometimes after a break, you go back and the ideas seem new and better."[7]

Since she has a flower garden at her house, Lowry tends to compare the process of writing a book to the process of composting. "I toss little tidbits of character and setting onto the compost heap in my mind and they ferment in the same way as my garbage and old tulip bulbs. Sometimes it stinks, but if I'm lucky, I'll end up with something productive."[8]

Lowry tends to become completely absorbed—morning, noon, and night—in the imaginary worlds of her novels. Says Lowry, "In a new novel, I work my way through the beginnings, creating the characters and setting, which will go on for a number of chapters and weeks. Once everything is in place, I get caught up in it. It's as if, now that the place and people are there, I've gone to live there. It's a very comfortable place to be, in the middle of that book, but it means that I'm living two lives. I have my daily life, where I have my house and my friends I go to the movies with, and children and grandchildren, but I'm also living in this other place. It's always there in my consciousness, and these other people are there, speaking to me."

She continued, "It's easier for me to write fiction. I like to use my imagination. Writing nonfiction kind of makes you stick to the truth.

Even though you can write nonfiction in creative and imaginative ways, for me that's not as much fun as writing stories."

Lowry says she writes for young people because she likes to help them answer their questions about who they are, where they are going, and how to relate to other people. She only writes about young protagonists because if she wrote in the voice of an adult, then she'd be writing an adult novel. "I don't think the writing process would be any different [if I wrote for adults], I don't think it's easier to write for kids. It's different, because you're seeing through the eyes of a child. Some people say they don't remember their childhood. Others say that when they think of it, they see it objectively, as if they were watching a film. But for me, it's as if I look through the eyes of the child I was then."[9]

As for choosing where her stories take place, Lowry sets most of her books in locations where she's lived—Pennsylvania, New York, and Maine—because she's most familiar with those settings. Lowry's book about surviving adolescence, *Autumn Street*, is set in the house in Carlisle, Pennsylvania, where she lived as a child before moving to Japan after the war.

For every book Lowry writes, there's research that needs to be done. For autobiographical books, the research is already done, and memory plays a large role. For fiction, much of the research happens in the library and in interviews with people who've had different experiences. For example, to research *Number the Stars*, a novel about a girl living in Denmark during World War II at a time when Jewish citizens were being relocated, Lowry traveled to Copenhagen and interviewed a Danish friend who'd been a child there in 1943, the time period of the novel. Lowry herself grew up at the same time, and her father fought in the war, but she was halfway across the world from Denmark. Her friend remembered wearing mittens to bed because there was no heat, and being hungry. She told Lowry about how, due to poor medical care and nutrition, her sister died while giving birth.

"But the most important thing," said Lowry, "was a story she told me, not about her own family, but about what really happened to all the people from Denmark during that time when the Jews were to be taken away by the Nazis and the Danish Christian population rose up as a group and hid and saved their Jewish population. And that seemed to me to be such an important story that I decided to write the book. Then of course I had to make up the plot and the characters. But the history was real and the importance of the piece of history is real."[10]

Lowry also read books about World War II and the Nazi occupation of Denmark for *Number the Stars*. When she visited Copenhagen, she talked to people who'd been adults in 1943, and spent time in the places she'd mentioned in the book. She wanted the book to include authentic descriptions of the landscape, so that it would seem more true to life. Finally, she gave early drafts of the novel to her Danish friends, then tried to incorporate their suggestions when revising.

Even though most of Lowry's characters are fictional, all of them are "real" in her mind from the first moment they reach the page, even if they are not based on people from Lowry's life. (In fact, most of Lowry's characters are not based on real people, with some exceptions; Anastasia Krupnik, who was loosely modeled on Amy Carter, and the characters from *Autumn Street*, which is mostly autobiographical, are all based on people from Lowry's life.)

Lowry knows how all of her characters dress, behave, talk, and react. She makes notes for minor characters, including small details. "For example," said Lowry in an interview, "right now I have on my desk a list of all the children in Sam Krupnik's nursery-school class. By looking at the list, I remind myself that Becky is a crybaby and Adam is a troublemaker. When those characters appear, they will behave according to those traits."[11] Becky and Adam are students in Sam Krupnik's class—they are only minor characters in Sam's stories, but Lowry still makes them vivid and true to life.

According to Lowry, "It would not serve my writing well to look for something topical or trendy, and then fashion a book about it. My books tend to be more character-driven. More often than not, I will feel a character begin to form in my imagination, and then things will happen to that character when I begin to write."[12]

Lowry doesn't believe she's ever written a flawless book, and doubts she ever will. "If I did, why write another?" But how does she know when a book is finished? Lowry says, "You simply begin to feel that it is done, or at least as done as you can make it. At that point, I do feel a sense of satisfaction and completeness—but it's a false sense, because if I read a published book six months later, or a year later, then I find things I wish I could change, things I feel I could make better."[13] This would be true, she said, even if she held onto a finished manuscript for a year, then revised it before turning it in to her publisher. "The best thing to do is finish, call it done, turn it in, and go on to the next book."

Lowry always writes the titles of her books last. "I think a good title should be fairly short, easy to remember, easy to say, and should tell something about the book without revealing too much,"[14] Lowry said in an interview.

The life of a successful novelist gets busier with every book. Lowry spends a lot of time making speeches at schools and universities, answering fan mail, and conducting interviews with magazines and school kids. These activities help promote, or publicize, her books. Oddly, she has less time to write because of her success as a writer.

# 3 Turning Memories into Books

In 1995, Lowry's son, Grey, who was a United States Air Force pilot, died in an airplane accident in Germany. Because it occurred while he was on a military mission, Grey's death became a media event. It was reported in magazine articles and on television news programs. Lowry received letters from people who wanted to express their sympathy, as well as share their own tragic stories. This experience convinced Lowry that writing stories plays an important role in grieving and coping, as well as in remembering. After Grey's death, she was inspired to write her autobiography, *Looking Back: A Book of Memories*. She wanted the world, including Grey's daughter, who was an infant at the time, to know what it was missing without her son in it.

"Grey left a daughter who was a year-and-a-half old. He adored her and I was very concerned that she wouldn't remember him. So I set out to create a little book for her about her short life with her father," said Lowry. In the process of gathering material, she came across hundreds of family photos. "Looking through all these pictures, triggered so many memories. It was my [reason] for putting these photographs together in some form."[1]

*Looking Back* is filled with photographs of Lowry's family and anecdotes from her childhood. The book also contains a few excerpts from her novels, which link certain episodes from Lowry's fiction to events that happened in her own life. For example, Lowry sometimes writes about having dogs as pets (and, in the case of *Stay!: Keeper's Story* [1990], she wrote a whole novel from a dog's point of view), which is an experience she knows first-hand, because she's has always had dogs as pets, even as a child. (By the way, the dog who lives with her now is a shaggy Tibetan terrier named Bandit.)

Lowry has said that she believes it's important for writers to have long and precise memories. "More than that, it has to be subjective as well. It incorporates the feelings that I was having. That's true, I think, of all my memories, and I think that's necessary in order to write. It's that I re-tell as I remember. I have no way of accounting for that. It's lucky."[2]

Lowry found that writing her own autobiography was simpler, in some ways, than writing fiction. "With a piece of fiction you have to shape a plot, think about foreshadowing, and tuck all the ends in," says Lowry. "I didn't have to worry about any of that with *Looking Back*. From the start I didn't pretend that this would be an organized thing. I sort of viewed this book as having the form that memory actually has—fragmented, disconnected, yet in the long run connecting in sometimes surprising ways."[3]

*Looking Back* chronicles the turning points of Lowry's life, including the deaths of her sister and her son, as well as everyday trivia, such as what kind of car she drives, her favorite food, and the names of her childhood pets. "No matter how uneventful a life may seem, there are many moments of enhanced emotion that do lend themselves to fiction."[4] After reading the intimate memoir and studying the old photographs it contains, one feels as if one has come to know Lowry personally, as one comes to know the characters in her books.

In an essay, Lowry wrote, "I deal with the frustrations, fears, and disappointments of life by making stories out of them: by examining them, tipping them upside down and inside out, arranging them in an order that makes sense, weaving them through with details and holding them up to the light."[5]

Lowry explained how her memories influence her fiction in her second Newbery Medal acceptance speech, which she won for *The Giver* in 1994:

I'd like to try to tell you the origins of this book. It is a little like Jonas looking into the river and realizing that it carried with it everything that has come from an Elsewhere. A spring, perhaps, at the beginning, bubbling up from the earth; then a trickle from a glacier, a mountain stream entering farther along; and each tributary bringing with it the collected bits and pieces from the past, from the distant, from the countless Elsewheres: all of it moving, mingled, in the current.

For me, the tributaries are memories, and I've selected only a few. I'll tell them to you chronologically. I have to go way back. I'm starting forty-six years ago. In 1948 I am eleven years old. I have gone with my mother, sister, and brother to join my father, who has been in Tokyo for two years and will be there for several more.

We live there, in the center of that huge Japanese city, in a small American enclave with a very American name: Washington Heights. We live in an American-style house, with American neighbors, and our little community has its own movie theater, which shows American movies, and a small church, a tiny library, and an elementary school; and in many ways it is an odd replica of a United States village.

(In later, adult years, I was to ask my mother why we lived there instead of taking advantage of the opportunity to live within the Japanese community and to learn and experience a different way of life. But she seemed surprised by my question. She said that we lived where we did because it was comfortable. It was familiar. It was safe.)

At eleven years old I am not a particularly adventurous child, nor am I rebellious one. But I have always been curious.

I have a bicycle. Again and again— countless times—without my parents' knowledge, I ride my bicycle out the back gate of the fence that surrounds our comfortable, familiar, safe American community. I ride down a hill because I am curious, and I enter, riding down that hill, an unfamiliar, slightly uncomfortable, perhaps even unsafe—though I never feel it to be—area of Tokyo that throbs with life.

It is a district called Shibuya. It is crowded with shops and people and theaters and street vendors and the day-to-day bustle of Japanese life.

I can remember, still, after all these years, the smells: fish and fertilizer and charcoal; the sounds: music and shouting and the clatter of wooden shoes and wooden sticks and wooden wheels; and the colors: I remember the babies and toddlers dressed in bright pink and orange and red, most of all; but I remember, too, the dark blue uniforms of the schoolchildren—the strangers who are my own age.

I wander through Shibuya day after day during those years when I am eleven, twelve, thirteen. I love the feel of it, the vigor and garish brightness and the noise: all such a contrast to my own life.

But I never talk to anyone. I am not frightened of the people, who are so different from me, but I am shy. I watch the children shouting and playing around a school, and they are children my age, and they watch me in return; but we never speak to one another.

One afternoon I am standing on a street corner when one woman near me reaches out, touches my hair, and says something. I back away, startled, because my knowledge of the language is poor and I misunderstand her words. I think she has said "kiraidesu," meaning that she dislikes me; and I am embarrassed, and confused, wondering what I have done wrong: how have I disgraced myself?

Then, after a moment, I realize my mistake. She has said, actually, 'kirei-desu.' She has called me pretty. And I look for her, in the crowd, at least to smile, perhaps to say thank you if I can overcome my shyness enough to speak. But she is gone.

I remember this moment—this instant of communication gone awry—again and again over the years. Perhaps this is where the river starts.

In 1954 and 1955, I am a college freshman living in a very small dormitory, actually a converted private home, with a group of perhaps fourteen other girls. We are very much alike. We wear the same sort of clothes: cashmere sweaters and plaid wool skirts, knee socks and loafers. We all smoke Marlboro cigarettes, and we knit—usually argyle socks for our boyfriends—and play bridge. Sometimes we study; and we get good grades because we are all the cream of the crop, the valedictorians and class presidents from our high schools all over the United States.

One of the girls in our dorm is not like the rest of us. She doesn't wear our uniform. She wears blue jeans instead of skirts, and she doesn't curl her hair or knit or play bridge. She doesn't date or go to fraternity parties and dances.

She's a smart girl, a good student, a pleasant enough person, but she is different, somehow alien, and that makes us uncomfortable. We react with a kind of mindless cruelty. We don't tease or torment her, but we do something worse: we ignore her. We pretend that she doesn't exist. In a small house of fourteen young women, we make one invisible.

Somehow, by shutting her out, we make ourselves feel comfortable. Familiar. Safe.

I think of her now and then as the years pass. Those thoughts—fleeting, but profoundly remorseful—enter the current of the river.

In the summer of 1979, I am sent by a magazine I am working for to an island off the coast of Maine to write an article about a painter who lives there alone. I spend a good deal of time with this man, and we talk a lot about color. It is clear to me that although I am a highly visual person—a person who sees and appreciates form and composition and color—this man's capacity for seeing color goes far beyond mine.

I photograph him while I am there, and I keep a copy of his photograph for myself because there is something about his face—his eyes—which haunts me.

Later I hear that he has become blind.

I think about him—his name is Carl Nelson—from time to time. His photograph hangs over my desk. I wonder what it was like for him to lose the colors about which he was so impassioned.

I wish, in a whimsical way, that he could have somehow magically given me the capacity to see the way he did.

A little bubble begins, a little spurt, which will trickle into the river.

In 1989, I go to a small village in Germany to attend the wedding of one of my sons. In an ancient church, he marries his Margret in a ceremony conducted in a language I do not speak and cannot understand.

But one section of the service is in English. A woman stands in the balcony of that old stone church and sings the words from the Bible: 'Where you go, I will go. Your people will be my people.'

How small the world has become, I think, looking around the church at the many people who sit there wishing happiness to my son and his new wife, wishing it in their own language as I am wishing it in mine. 'We are all each other's people now,' I find myself thinking.

Can you feel that this memory is a stream that is now entering the river?[6]

Lowry also wrote about the importance of memory in creating fiction in her autobiography:

We come into their world on our own—in Hawaii, as I did, or New York, or China, or Africa, or Montana—and we leave it in the same way, on our own, wherever we happen to be at the time—in a plane, in our beds, in a car, in a space shuttle, or in a field of flowers.

And between those times, we try to connect along the way with others who are also on their own.

If we're lucky, we have a mother who reads to us.

We have a teacher or two along the way who make us feel special.

We have dogs who do the stupid dog tricks we teach them and who lie on our bed when we're not looking, because it smells like us, and so we pretend not to notice the paw prints on the bedspread.

We have friends who lend us their favorite books.

Maybe we have children, and grandchildren, and funny mailmen, and eccentric great-aunts, and uncles who can pull pennies out of our ears.

All of them teach us stuff. They teach us about combustion engines and the major products of Bolivia, and what poems are not boring, and how to be kind to each other, and how to laugh . . . and when we just have to make the best of things even though it is hard sometimes.

Looking back together, telling our stories to one another, we learn how to be on our own.[7]

# 4 Lowry's Books

L ois Lowry has written sad books, funny books, books about boys and books about girls, long books and not-so-long books. She has written autobiographical books, fictional books, and books set in futuristic societies. If you'd like to read more of Lowry's books, but you're not sure which ones you'd like (since she's written so many different kinds), you can read the following summaries to decide which ones—if not all of them—you'd most enjoy.

Lowry's first novel, *A Summer to Die*, which was published in 1977, is about a thirteen-year-old girl named Meg and her older sister Molly, whom Meg alternately admires and resents. Molly is dying of leukemia. (Though the book is not autobiographical, Lois Lowry's own sister died of cancer when they were both in their twenties, and she drew from her own feelings of grief to make the book more authentic.) *A Summer to Die* was loved by reviewers and readers alike. A review in *Horn Book Magazine* called the book "a well-crafted reaffirmation of universal values,"[1] and a *Publishers Weekly* article called it "a marvelous book and a help in understanding loss."[2]

Near the close of the book, Meg reflects on the cycle of life and death: "Time goes on, and your life is still there, and you have to live it. After a while you remember the good things more often than the bad. Then, gradually, the empty silent parts of you fill up with sounds of talking and laughter again, and the jagged edges of sadness are softened by memories."[3]

A review in *School Library Journal* praised the book for capturing the mysteries of living and dying without influencing readers' emotions, and for providing understanding and a comforting sense of completion. Another review stated that "this remarkable American first novel presents most sensitively and convincingly an intelligent thirteen-year-old's reactions to and gradual awareness and acceptance of the fact that her more beautiful, more popular older sister will die of leukemia at the end of their summer in the country. The family relationships are closely, often humorously, observed."[4]

Another of Lowry's more serious books is *Find a Stranger, Say Goodbye*, published in 1978, in which an adopted girl named Natalie searches for her biological parents. In the end, Natalie must accept the fact that despite the journey she's taken to find her own identity, she is still the same girl, with the same loving, supportive family. One might conclude that Lowry's message, in the book, is that the love of one's family has nothing to do with biological connection. Natalie loves her parents not because they gave her life, but because they've cared for her since she was born.

In *Autumn Street*, a solemn and realistic portrayal of adolescence published in 1979, Lowry explores the dark themes of death and illness. A review of the book in the *School Library Journal* said that *Autumn Street* was "obviously for mature readers" and called the book "a reading experience that touches the heart."[5]

When Lowry began writing about a spunky and clever ten-year-old named Anastasia Krupnik, she was looking to take a break from writing sad, serious stories. "I needed to cheer up a bit," she said. "I was writing too much serious stuff, too many sad things, and so I just decided to write a lighthearted book, and I created Anastasia."[6]

Lowry intended to write only a short story starring Anastasia, but at the end, she liked the character and her family so much that she decided to continue, and the Anastasia books have become Lowry's best-known works. Unlike her serious novels, the Anastasia books are lighthearted in tone. Anastasia's parents are caring and wise, and they always have plenty of time to help Anastasia work through her problems.

In the first book, *Anastasia Krupnik*, which was published in 1979, ten-year-old Anastasia lists all the things she loves and hates, and develops an obsession with naming her new baby brother. She also complains about her own name, saying that if she had her name stenciled onto a T-shirt, the letters would go all the way up into her armpits.

A review of *Anastasia Krupnik* in *Booklist*, another important publishing magazine, stated that Lowry "masterfully captures the heart and mind of a perceptive fourth-grader. Anastasia, age ten, keeps track, in a green notebook, of the important things that happen to her, including a (changing) list entitled 'Things I hate/Things I love.'"[7]

*Anastasia Again!*, the second book featuring Anastasia, was published in 1981. In it, Anastasia must cope with her family's move to the suburbs. She's angry that her parents decided to move without consulting her about it, but once she's there, she grows to like it. Slowly. In a review of the book for *Horn Book Magazine*, Mary M. Burns wrote, "Anastasia Krupnik is one of the most intriguing [interesting] female protagonists to appear in children's books . . . Genuinely funny, the novel is a marvelously human portrait of an articulate adolescent."[8] A review for the *School Library Journal*, stated that "Lowry has the ability to describe common experiences and situations in an uncommon and [lively] manner, while at the same time providing easy access for readers who will undoubtedly find that many of Anastasia's notions bear a close relation to their own."[9]

Reading is as important to Anastasia as it was to Lowry when she was a girl. *Anastasia at Your Service*, published in 1982, is the third book about Anastasia Krupnik. This time around, twelve-year-old Anastasia tackles boredom, the blues, and the frustration of depending on her parents for money. Feeling sorry for herself, she acts out the farewell scenes from Louisa May Alcott's classic story about four sisters, *Little Women*, and Shakespeare's romantic play, *Romeo and Juliet*.

In *Taking Care of Terrific*, which was published in 1983, the main protagonist, fourteen-year-old Enid Irene Crowley, resembles Anastasia in that she is energetic and mature for her age. She's also very funny. Unlike Anastasia, however, Enid's parents are generally absent—they both work all the time. Enid and her friend Seth are rather mature for their age; they joke about becoming addicted to drugs (though they never try drugs), but end up in only minor trouble with their parents. Lowry portrays this dysfunctional family as humorously as she does the Krupniks' functional family.

Lowry explores a different kind of family in *The One Hundredth Thing About Caroline*, which was published in 1983. Eleven-year-old Caroline enjoys a close relationship with her mother, who is a single parent. Like Anastasia and Enid, Caroline is smart and mature—she already knows that she wants to be a vertebrate paleontologist specializing in Mesozoic era dinosaurs. Her hostility toward her pesky older brother, J. P., and toward her father, who lives in another city, are explored further in the sequel, *Switcharound*, published in 1985.

In *Anastasia, Ask Your Analyst*, published in 1984, Anastasia must mate her gerbils for her seventh-grade science project. She also becomes convinced that she requires a psychiatrist to deal with her many anxieties and questions. Instead of taking her to a psychiatrist, her parents buy her a book of essays by Sigmund Freud, the famous psychoanalyst. The problem, Anastasia explains, is her hormones, which are causing all sorts of physical and emotional changes.

In *Us and Uncle Fraud*, also published in 1984, the main character is eleven-year-old Louise Cunningham, whose Uncle Claude has arrived at her family's house for a brief stay. The Cunninghams are a loving family, but Louise's father has a hard time showing his emotions until his oldest son comes close to dying in an accident.

The fifth Anastasia book, *Anastasia on Her Own*, was published in 1985. In this story, Anastasia must take care of the household chores while her mother goes to California on business for ten days. When unexpected obstacles arise, Anastasia learns that running a house isn't as easy as it looks, and she becomes more understanding of her mother and more compassionate. In the next book, *Anastasia Has the Answers*, published in 1986, Anastasia is humiliated when she can't climb the rope in gym class; she practices diligently to prove herself. A year later, *Anastasia's Chosen Career* was published. In this book, Anastasia, at age thirteen, takes modeling classes to improve her self-esteem.

"Lowry gives readers a fine mixture of wit and wisdom," a reviewer wrote in 1987. "She offer[s] funny adolescent dialogue that is true to their interests and language, and the insight of an affectionate and perceptive observer of the human scene."[10]

Caroline's older brother J. P. shows up again in 1990 as the main character of *Your Move, J. P.!* In this book, J. P., who is in seventh grade, makes the mistake of telling tall tales to impress the object of his first crush, a lovely classmate named Angela Galsworthy. About this book, *Horn Book Magazine* stated, "The author makes the most of the humor in J. P.'s antics but maintains a rueful [apologetic] sympathy throughout for his plight [situation] and for his eventual admission of the truth."[11] Another review said that, "Lowry's story is awash in real emotion yet able to make fun of itself at the same time."[12]

*Number the Stars*, which was published in 1990, is a work of historical fiction, which means that it is a fictional story set in a real historical setting. In the novel, ten-year-old Annemarie Johansen and her family protect Annemarie's Jewish friend Ellen from the Nazis by disguising her as Annemarie's late sister. The story is told from Annemarie's point of view, so the horrors of living in wartime are mixed in with the challenges faced by ten-year-olds everywhere. Annemarie worries about school and friends even as the war goes on around her.

*Number the Stars* is a gloomy story, but Lowry said that she didn't cry while writing it. The book did make her sad, though, because a tragedy occurs near the end. Lowry has no plans to write another novel based on historical facts, though she hasn't ruled out the possibility.

The worlds depicted in *The Giver* (1994), and *Gathering Blue* (2000), are dystopias—societies in which everything is controlled for evil purposes. In a utopia, everything is controlled for the collective good. Utopias and dystopias exist mostly in books and movies, though real-life communities that attempt to create ideal living conditions for their members have always existed all over the world.

In *Gathering Blue*, the main character, Kira, is a young girl who has the power to weave beautiful fabrics, and who lives in a strange fictional world. In an interview with Tammy Currier of Teenreads.com, a Web site that reviews books for teenagers, Lowry said, "The artist is always the 'outsider' in mainstream society—the one who peeks beyond the edges of the known, the one who explores, who takes risks. Often, I think, this is not a role one chooses, but rather the role that somehow one is chosen for. This is true of Kira in *Gathering Blue*. Her talent appears, unbidden. Then having been gifted in that way, as true artists are, she has the choice of how to use the gift, as true artists always do. Some sell out and some opt for the easy success, as Kira could. Others choose the harder way, the way that may make a greater difference in the world."[13]

Reviewers agree that Lowry's futuristic tales are richly imagined and told. A *Horn Book Magazine* review pointed out that Lowry's dystopic novels are a large departure from her other books not only because they don't include rich and vivid characters living in contemporary families, but also because Lowry has, in *The Giver* and *Gathering Blue*, created subtext [a second layer of meaning] by using innuendo, foreshadowing, and resonance. Innuendo is a subtle insinuation, or hint; foreshadowing is suggesting an event that comes later in a story; and resonance happens when one part of a story increases the meaning of another part, and vice versa.

"Take, for example, the opening sentence [of *The Giver*]," wrote Patty Campbell in the *Horn Book Magazine* review. "'It was almost December, and Jonas was beginning to be frightened.' The word December is loaded with resonance: the darkness of the solstice, endings, Christmas, cold. *Almost* and *beginning* pull forward to the future source of his fear . . . The name Jonas, too, is evocative—of the biblical Jonah, he who is sent by God to cry against the wickedness of Nineveh, an unwilling lone messenger with a mission that will be received with hostility. In one seemingly simple sentence, Lowry sets the mood and direction of her story, foreshadows its outcome, and plants an irresistible narrative pull."[14]

Another review of *The Giver* and *Gathering Blue* noted that "Because Lowry constructs alternative and complex societies in each book, we can use them as the [reason] for students to examine our own society and those of other countries."[15] In another review of *Gathering Blue* in *Horn Book Magazine*, Roger Sutton claimed that Lowry's unemotional writing style works well because it is understated, and that the story's even pace highlights the chaotic nature of the fictional world.[16]

Lowry was inspired to write *The Giver* after visiting her father in a nursing home. Her father had lost much of his long-term memory, and Lowry began thinking that without memory, there is no such thing as emotional pain. She envisioned a world where the past is forgotten deliberately. "The whole concept of memory interests me a great deal," said Lowry. "I've always been fascinated by the thought of what memory is and what it does and how it works and what we learn from it."[17]

Lowry considers *The Giver* her most complicated book, because the world where it is set is entirely imaginary, but *Autumn Street* is her favorite. She says that the reason why is because the characters in the book were real people—most of whom were very dear to her. Lowry has said that the character named Elizabeth in that book was autobiographical; the character Meg in *A Summer to Die* was also autobiographical.

Her favorite character, though, is Sweet Hosanna from *Rabble Starkey*. She's the mother of the main character. Lowry is also particularly fond of Anastasia's mother. In an interview published by Scholastic Press, she said, "Maybe I'm just fond of mothers because I am one."[18]

## A Note of Controversy

As mentioned before, Lowry won the Newbery Medal two times—for *Number the Stars* in 1990 and *The Giver* in 1994. But *The Giver*, which is generally considered Lowry's most ambitious book, is also her most controversial novel. It is frequently included in the American Library Association's list of banned and challenged books; in 2000, *The Giver* appeared on that list alongside J. K. Rowling's Harry Potter books, which were cited for occult and Satanic themes; John Steinbeck's *Of Mice and Men*, for offensive language, racism, and violence; and Maya Angelou's *I Know Why the Caged Bird Sings*, for explicit portrayal of rape and sexual abuse.

People have complained that *The Giver* is too religious, or not religious enough. The novel has been called un-American, too spiritual, and too pessimistic. In an interview with *Boston Globe Magazine*, Lowry tried to guess what about

*The Giver* inspires so much controversy. "It's unclear," she said. "I think what bothers people—but nobody actually says this—is that a twelve-year-old child who has been dutifully obeying all the clearly defined rules of society said, in effect, 'Halt. I've got to break the rules in order to put an end to all this evil.'"[19]

About the restricted society in *The Giver*, Lowry said in an interview, "It relates to me the same way it relates to everybody—it is a reminder of the importance of the choices we make; also, the value of our freedom to make choices."

The ending of *The Giver* is somewhat ambiguous, meaning that it can be interpreted in a few different ways. This has inspired even more controversy. Lowry has this to say about the ending: "[Jonah] takes food because he needs to survive and he knows that. He takes the bicycle because he needs to hurry and the bike is faster than legs. And he takes the baby because he is going out to create a future. And babies always represent the future in the same way children represent the future to adults. And so Jonas takes the baby so the baby's life will be saved, but he takes the baby also in order to begin again with a new life."[20]

In her second Newbery Medal acceptance speech, in 1994, Lowry shared some of her readers' interpretations of the ending of *The Giver*. A sixth grader said, "I think that when they were traveling, they were traveling in a circle. When they came to Elsewhere, it was their old community, but they had accepted the memories and all the feelings that go along with it."

Another reader said, "Jonas was kind of like Jesus because he took pain for everyone else in the community so they wouldn't have to suffer. And, at the very end of the book, when Jonas and Gabe reached the place they knew as Elsewhere, you described Elsewhere as if it were Heaven."

A seventh-grade reader said, "I was really surprised that they just died in the end. That was a bummer. You could have made them stay alive, I thought."

Finally, another reader said, "A lot of people I know would hate that ending, but not me. I loved it. Mainly because I got to make the book happy. I decided they would make it. They made it to the past. I decided the past was our world, and the future was their world. It was parallel worlds."[21]

With *The Giver*, Lowry didn't intend to surprise her readers or cause controversy. As she put it, "*The Giver* is many things to many different people. People bring to it their own complicated sense of beliefs and hopes and dreams and fears and all of that. So I don't want to put my own feelings into it, my own beliefs, and ruin that for people who create their own endings in their minds. I will say that I find it an optimistic ending."[22]

A few of Lowry's books have been made into movies, musicals, or plays. *Find a Stranger, Say Goodbye* was made into a television After School Special in 1980. The program was called "I Don't Know Who I Am." *Anastasia at Your Service* was recorded on audiocassette by Learning Library in 1984. Perhaps Lowry's favorite adaptation was the musical version of *Number the Stars*, which she saw in New York.

# 5 A Word of Advice

In an interview for Write4kids.com, Lowry listed the key elements of a novel:

1. Character
2. Quest
3. Complications and Choices
4. Catastrophe
5. Conclusion
6. Change

Lowry claims that a writer should write a story first, then see how and where it fits this pattern. It doesn't work to do things in reverse order, to try and fit a story to the pattern. You should write a story, she says, by pretending that you're telling a story to a friend. "It should be an intimate and private telling, friend to friend," says Lowry. "It should be YOU, laughing, crying, teasing, angry, relating events, inviting your close friend to pay attention, to empathize." Empathy is when one person understands another person's experiences. "This will be your voice, a recognizable one."[1]

Lowry's own voice, or writing style, is very natural and straightforward, which makes her books easy to read but difficult to put down. About her writing style, Lowry's editor and friend Walter Lorraine wrote, in an article for *Horn Book Magazine*, that there is a meter and rhythm to Lowry's writing style that makes it uniquely accessible, which means it's easy to read. "With many writers," said Lorraine, "it takes the reader, at least a clumsy reader like me, half a chapter or so because he becomes comfortable with the style . . . With Lois one sentence draws you immediately into the world of the story. There is an instinctive feel for the way all those word sounds are woven into a rhythmic whole."[2]

Lowry believes that the best way to make yourself write—which, you may recall, she does for several hours every day—is to genuinely love writing. No matter what your vocation, or job, it will come more naturally if you enjoy doing it. "I can't imagine any place that I'd rather be than right here, at my desk," she said in her 1994 Newbery Medal acceptance speech. "I need self-discipline to make me get up and take the dog for a walk, or to cook dinner!"[3]

And though, for Lowry, writing has never become boring or discouraging, sometimes her work is exhausting. About being a writer, Lowry says, "I love the people I meet—the children, writers, librarians, teachers, who all have the same interests I do. I love the process of putting words on a page, rearranging them, making them work somehow, hearing them slip into a sequence that sounds right."

Lowry doesn't keep a journal, though she writes e-mail daily. She gets ideas for fiction "everywhere, all the time," as she has said. "Phrases, fragments, small snippets of dialogue, the face (or name) of a character. Something visual: the way the light falls on a porch; the walk and posture of a stranger. For me (for all writers, I'm certain) the world is a constant barrage of the imagination. And words, too. If you'll forgive the overly personal reference here: When my son was killed recently, I received that terrible news on the telephone, at 5:30 A.M., awakened from sleep. The phrase 'ruined dawn' appeared in my mind then and has been there ever since. Is that an 'idea'? Not really. But it is a concept which is so strong I know eventually it will write itself somewhere."[4]

"I always tell children that they should write letters to their grandparents," says Lowry, "and they groan when I say that. But I don't mean it as a joke.

The best way to write fiction is to write it as if you're telling a story to a friend. Getting in the habit of writing letters to friends or grandparents is a great way to practice writing fiction. The best fiction has that kind of intimate quality to it. And, if you're not in the habit of writing with that warmth and intimacy, then your fiction becomes stilted."[5]

Reading, too, makes a big difference in the life of a writer. "If I read brilliant paragraphs, then I want to rush off and write brilliant paragraphs."

Any more advice to young writers? Don't focus on becoming a published author, she says. Instead, Lowry recommends fostering a love for language, writing, and stories. "It bothers me a lot, to hear kids talk about publishing and all its accoutrements—agents and contracts and rejection slips. None of that has anything to do with love of language, which is the essential ingredient for a writer."[6]

There's one more essential ingredient in Lowry's recipe for becoming an author. "The one thing all writers need is solitude," she told the *Boston Globe Magazine*. "I like sitting alone in my office, using my imagination as my only company and my only conversation being that of fictional characters. I never feel lonely when I'm writing, although of course, I do it all alone. I love the excitement of arranging words on a page, moving them around, testing them out, listening to their sounds and feeling their meaning. All of that process is very satisfying to me."[7]

Lois Lowry is truly a lucky woman. She always knew what she wanted to do when she grew up. From age three, when she learned to read and write before other kids her age, through to nursery school, when her teacher told her parents of her talent, through college, when she studied writing, and all the way into adulthood, when she used her kids' nap times to write, Lowry knew she was meant to be a writer. And because of her unique ability to portray realistic and endearing characters, many young readers fell in love with her books, and she succeeded as an author. She continues to write every day in an office in her home, as well as pursue other favorite activities, like going to movies and tending her garden.

Remember the two predictions from the Chinese fortune cookies that Lowry carries around in her wallet? One said, "YOU WILL BECOME FAMOUS IN A FAR-OUT PROFESSION," and the other said, "YOU WILL ATTEND A PARTY WHERE STRANGE CUSTOMS PREVAIL." Well, at the close of her Newbery Medal speech in 1990, Lowry admitted that the first fortune had originally predicted that she would become rich and famous in a far-out profession, but she'd changed it. "I didn't feel comfortable with the word rich," she said. "But of course it does have a meaning beyond the mundane world of royalties. Let's [give it] that meaning tonight, and say that my Chinese fortune—the unedited version—really did come true, because I feel immensely rich here with all of you—rich with the affection and the support you have all given me for a very long time, even before this party full of not-so-strange customs took place."[8]

Not everyone can be as fortunate as Lois Lowry, but surely everyone can apply the lessons she's taught—through her books and through her real life—to their own goals and pursuits. More than discipline, more than talent, and more than skill, Lois Lowry encourages by example to spend a lifetime pursuing what you love. In her case, the pursuit is writing.

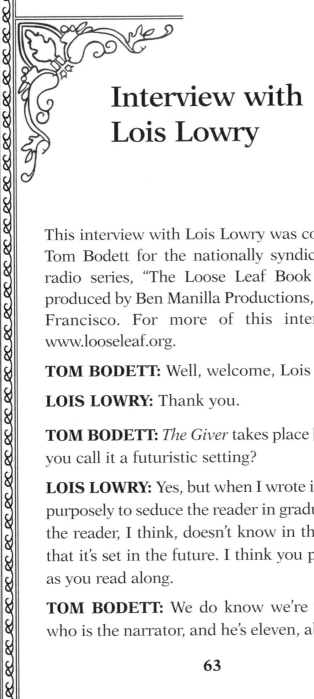

# Interview with Lois Lowry

This interview with Lois Lowry was conducted by Tom Bodett for the nationally syndicated public radio series, "The Loose Leaf Book Company," produced by Ben Manilla Productions, Inc., of San Francisco. For more of this interview, visit www.looseleaf.org.

**TOM BODETT:** Well, welcome, Lois Lowry.

**LOIS LOWRY:** Thank you.

**TOM BODETT:** *The Giver* takes place [in]—would you call it a futuristic setting?

**LOIS LOWRY:** Yes, but when I wrote it, I intended purposely to seduce the reader in gradually, so that the reader, I think, doesn't know in the beginning that it's set in the future. I think you perceive that as you read along.

**TOM BODETT:** We do know we're with Jonas, who is the narrator, and he's eleven, about to turn twelve. And turning twelve has some significance here in this community.

**LOIS LOWRY:** Yes, it has a great deal of significance. Do you want me to try to explain that?

**TOM BODETT:** Yeah.

**LOIS LOWRY:** Well, in this world of the future, and it takes place in quite a small community, otherwise this wouldn't have worked, all the children turn twelve at the same time. And at that time, they're given their assignment for their remaining rest of their life. So when they turn twelve, they're told what they are going to be. And from that time on, they're training, and their education is directed toward that. So it's a time, when they're eleven, when they're all apprehensive, as Jonas says, and excited, and trying to imagine what's in store for them. And that's when the book opens, that's what Jonas is thinking about.

**TOM BODETT:** Yeah, and some of them, they're pretty sure they're going to be nurturers or basically I guess nursery workers, or some of them will care for the elderly, some will be recreational directors. Jonas doesn't really have much of a clue about what he's going to be. He thinks a lot, which is maybe our first clue to Jonas. And he has something else going on, too, where you address this, the adolescent puberty issue. They call it the stirring.

**LOIS LOWRY:** Yeah, that is introduced a little later, but not too much later. And of course, it's common to kids at that age, but in this world, where everything is quite controlled, the children have no idea what stirrings mean or are. And in fact, when they begin to experience this, as Jonas does, they are immediately given medication so they don't feel it any longer. And that's your first clue, really, that the world they live in is devoid of any real depth of feelings.

**TOM BODETT:** Yeah, and it's not as if they think of it even as evil. It's just like, Oh, you have the stirrings, here's what you do, you start taking these pills now.

**LOIS LOWRY:** Yeah, right.

**TOM BODETT:** And so the young people really never even know what it is.

**LOIS LOWRY:** They don't know what they're missing.

**TOM BODETT:** Why don't we work our way up to his ceremony of twelve, when he is given his assignment, which is really something quite exceptional and unexpected.

**LOIS LOWRY:** Yes. He's held out to the last. They jump over him when they give the assignments. And finally, when he's the only one left, and very nervous, because he's been omitted, they call him forward, and explain to him that he's to be the new receiver, the receiver of memories. And that he's been given this assignment because of his unusual capacities, which include what they call the ability to see beyond.

**TOM BODETT:** Yes, and the way it works is the Giver, who is a kindly old man, lays his hands on Jonas, and he kind of receives these memories telepathically somehow. And it starts off, let me read this passage:

"Jonas obeyed. He closed his eyes waiting, and felt the hands again. Then he felt the warmth again, the sunshine again, coming from the sky of this other consciousness that was so new to him. This time, as he lay basking in the wonderful warmth, he felt the passage of time. His real self was aware that it was only a minute or two, but his other memory receiving self felt hours pass in the sun. His skin began to sting. Restlessly, he moved one arm, bending it, and felt the sharp pain in the crease of his inner arm at the elbow. 'Ouch!' he said, loudly, and shifted on the bed. 'Ow,' he said, wincing at the shift, and even moving his mouth to speak made his face hurt."

So, Lois, this is his first painful memory of sunburn.

**LOIS LOWRY:** Yeah, something we've all experienced from time to time. It's a small thing, but it's his introduction to pain.

ew receiver, the receiver of
een given this assignment
acities, which include what
eyond.

e way it works is the Giver,
s his hands on Jonas, and
memories telepathically
et me read this passage:
ed his eyes waiting, and
ne felt the warmth again,
from the sky of this other
ew to him. This time, as
erful warmth, he felt the
If was aware that it was
other memory receiving
His skin began to sting.
, bending it, and felt the
inner arm at the elbow.
hifted on the bed. 'Ow,'
, and even moving his
e hurt."

ful memory of sunburn.

g we've all experienced
nall thing, but it's his

# Interview with Lois Lowry

This interview with Lois Lowry was conducted by Tom Bodett for the nationally syndicated public radio series, "The Loose Leaf Book Company," produced by Ben Manilla Productions, Inc., of San Francisco. For more of this interview, visit www.looseleaf.org.

**TOM BODETT:** Well, welcome, Lois Lowry.

**LOIS LOWRY:** Thank you.

**TOM BODETT:** *The Giver* takes place [in]—would you call it a futuristic setting?

**LOIS LOWRY:** Yes, but when I wrote it, I intended purposely to seduce the reader in gradually, so that the reader, I think, doesn't know in the beginning that it's set in the future. I think you perceive that as you read along.

**TOM BODETT:** We do know we're with Jonas, who is the narrator, and he's eleven, about to turn twelve. And turning twelve has some significance here in this community.

**LOIS LOWRY:** Yes, it has a great deal of significance. Do you want me to try to explain that?

**TOM BODETT:** Yeah.

**LOIS LOWRY:** Well, in this world of the future, and it takes place in quite a small community, otherwise this wouldn't have worked, all the children turn twelve at the same time. And at that time, they're given their assignment for their remaining rest of their life. So when they turn twelve, they're told what they are going to be. And from that time on, they're training, and their education is directed toward that. So it's a time, when they're eleven, when they're all apprehensive, as Jonas says, and excited, and trying to imagine what's in store for them. And that's when the book opens, that's what Jonas is thinking about.

**TOM BODETT:** Yeah, and some of them, they're pretty sure they're going to be nurturers or basically I guess nursery workers, or some of them will care for the elderly, some will be recreational directors. Jonas doesn't really have much of a clue about what he's going to be. He thinks a lot, which is maybe our first clue to Jonas. And he has something else going on, too, where you address this, the adolescent puberty issue. They call it the stirring.

to him that he's to be the memories. And that he's because of his unusual cap they call the ability to see

**TOM BODETT:** Yes, and t who is a kindly old man, la he kind of receives thes somehow. And it starts off,

"Jonas obeyed. He cl felt the hands again. Then the sunshine again, comin consciousness that was so he lay basking in the won passage of time. His real s only a minute or two, but h self felt hours pass in the su Restlessly, he moved one a sharp pain in the crease of 'Ouch!' he said, loudly, anc he said, wincing at the sh mouth to speak made his fa

So, Lois, this is his first p

**LOIS LOWRY:** Yeah, somet from time to time. It's a introduction to pain.

**TOM BODETT:** Jonas up until this point never realized that he was confined in any way, until he starts receiving these memories, which include a world which is much richer, and I would say more engaging to him than the one he lives in.

**LOIS LOWRY:** Yes. And yet the one he lives in has been a very comfortable world, and that makes it tough on him, because he knows that discomfort is part of the deeper and profounder world that has become more important to him. In terms of imprisonment, it's interesting that the community he lives in has no walls, but they're imprisoned there, nonetheless. They're victims of a set of rules that have been in existence for so long that it never occurs to anybody to disobey. And when Jonas realizes he has to leave there, that's a tough move for him.

**TOM BODETT:** And I read it was that sort of same kind of chilled satisfaction that—you know I read *1984*, you know Orwell's *1984*—back when I was a young kid sort of trying to figure out how I was going to bust out of this world and move on. And I would imagine that a kid could really relate to Jonas, although their worlds certainly are not in black and white, and they have a lot more choices than they probably think they do. Don't you think that any twelve-year-old or fifteen-year-old kid reading this story is going to feel like Jonas?

**LOIS LOWRY:** I would think they would love it when he gets on that bike and rides away. After I wrote this book, *The Giver*, I then began to think back to a period in my own life when I was exactly Jonas's age. Circumstances had taken me to live with my family in Tokyo, post-war Tokyo. I'm so old, that this was just after World War II. And my father's work was in Tokyo, and so off we went. And we lived, me twelve years old, and my family, in a little enclave that was entirely populated by Americans. And there was literally a wall around it. And inside that wall, we lived like Americans. We had a little movie theater that showed American movies, and we had a little library filled with American books. I did go out of that enclave each day to school. A bus came in, inside the wall, picked me and my pals up, and we went out into Tokyo to school, and then we came back to the safety behind our wall.

And within that little world, we were comfortable and safe, and everything was orderly, and outside the wall was the world of post-war Tokyo, which was so fascinating to me as a child. And my parents didn't know this at the time. They would have been horrified, had they known. But like Jonas, I got on my bike again and again, and rode out that gate, and roamed around Tokyo. Nineteen forty whatever it was. It was quite safe in those days to do that, for a child, and I was the only blonde kid in these vast residential areas of Japanese people. And it was a way of escaping from a kind of imprisonment that my parents had inflicted on me with the best of intentions. They thought that to live within this walled area would be to keep me safe and comfortable. And yet to this day, I wish that they had chosen to live out in the Japanese community, where I would have been exposed to a much richer cultural life.

**TOM BODETT:** Well that's an interesting piece of this. So Jonas is in a very similar circumstance. We don't really know what the world around this community is, but just like your childhood in Tokyo, everything is very controlled, and he is safe. And he doesn't even think to wonder what's outside, until he's given the memories. I suppose you might not have been too curious either, if you didn't see it through the bus window every day.

**LOIS LOWRY:** Exactly, exactly. And of course, in those days, we had no television. Our life in those days and in that place was very restrictive. So I don't know, I just kind of see that analogy between me and Jonas. I certainly didn't set out on my bicycle to save the world from which I had emerged. But as he rides out of the community and begins to experience the things that are beyond, I just make that analogy to myself, riding out and looking around with those great, curious eyes of childhood.

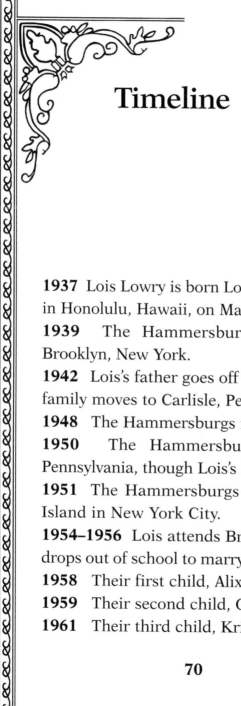

# Timeline

**1937** Lois Lowry is born Lois Ann Hammersburg in Honolulu, Hawaii, on March 20.

**1939** The Hammersburg family moves to Brooklyn, New York.

**1942** Lois's father goes off to World War II. The family moves to Carlisle, Pennsylvania.

**1948** The Hammersburgs move to Japan.

**1950** The Hammersburgs move back to Pennsylvania, though Lois's father stays in Japan.

**1951** The Hammersburgs move to Governor's Island in New York City.

**1954–1956** Lois attends Brown University, then drops out of school to marry Donald Grey Lowry.

**1958** Their first child, Alix, is born.

**1959** Their second child, Grey, is born.

**1961** Their third child, Kristin, is born.

**1962** Their fourth child, Benjamin, is born. Lois's sister Helen dies of cancer.

**1963** The Lowry family moves to Maine.

**1972** Lois earns her bachelor's degree from the University of Maine.

**1977** Lois's first novel, *A Summer to Die*, is published. She and her husband divorce.

**1979** Lois moves to Boston, Massachusetts.

**1990** Lois receives her first Newbery Medal for *Number the Stars*.

**1994** Lois receives another Newbery Medal for *The Giver*.

**1995** The Lowrys' son, Grey, dies in an airplane accident in Germany.

**2000** *The Giver* appears on the American Library Association's list of banned or challenged books.

# Selected Reviews from *School Library Journal*

## The Giver
**May 1993**

Gr 6-9—In a complete departure from her other novels, Lowry has written an intriguing story set in a society that is uniformly run by a Committee of Elders. Twelve-year-old Jonas's confidence in his comfortable "normal" existence as a member of this well-ordered community is shaken when he is assigned his life's work as the Receiver. The Giver, who passes on to Jonas the burden of being the holder for the community of all memory "back and back and back," teaches him the cost of living in an environment that is "without color, pain, or past." The tension leading up to the Ceremony, in which children are promoted not to another grade but to another stage in their life, and the drama and responsibility of the sessions with the Giver are gripping. The final flight for survival is as riveting as it is inevitable. The author makes real abstract concepts, such as the meaning of a life in which there are virtually no choices to be made and no experiences with deep feelings. This tightly plotted story and its believable characters will stay with readers for a long time. —Amy Kellman, The Carnegie Library of Pittsburgh, Pennsylvania

## *Taking Care of Terrific*
## April 1983

Gr 6-9—For her summer art course, Enid Crowley, fourteen, decides to sketch each day in the Public Garden where, once she's secretly changed her name to the more mellifluous "Cynthia," she intends to find romance, intrigue, danger and pathos. With her four-year-old charge, Joshua Warwick Cameron IV, who wants to change his name to Tom Terrific, Enid finds all those things and more in the course of the summer. It begins when Enid, Tom Terrific and Hawk, a black saxaphonist they've met at the Public Garden, organize the shopping bag ladies who hang out at the Garden into a protest to force the popsicle seller to carry root beer popsicles. Heady with the success of that campaign, and joined by Enid's new romantic interest Seth Sandroff, they decide to fulfill another dream they have for not only the shopping bag ladies, but also for overprotected Tom Terrific: to provide a midnight Swan Boat ride for the whole entourage. Acquiring both boat and the child at such an hour, however, involves some illegalities, as the group of dreamers is eventually made to realize. But it's fun while it lasts, and as always, Lowry's characters are memorable, including the Crowley's housekeeper, Mrs. Kolodny; Tom Terriffic's smothering mother; and Seth's ever-absent mother, pop psychologist Wilma Sandroff. This is a warm and poignant story that involves readers long beyond the first reading. —Susan F. Marcus, Pollard Middle School, Needham, Massachusetts

### *The One Hundredth Thing About Caroline*
### October 1983

Gr 5-7—Eleven-year-old Caroline is pretty much your average child; she has a mother who persists in serving weird vegetables at dinner and an obnoxious older brother, J. P., who is a self-proclaimed genius. What isn't average about Caroline is that Frederick Fiske, the mysterious man who lives upstairs, is plotting to kill both her and J. P.—at least, that's what Caroline and her chum Stacy think. While Stacy, a would-be investigative reporter who speaks in headlines ("Slayer Stalks Tots"), keeps herself busy gathering clues, Caroline frantically tries to squelch her mother's growing friendship with Fiske, and even J. P. gets into the act as he plans a high-voltage defense. The real explanation behind all this may be obvious to some, but many young readers will be kept in suspense right up to the climactic scene at a dinner party, which is both tense and humorous. As demonstrated in her *Anastasia* books (Houghton), Lowry's style is bright, fast-paced and funny, with skillfully-drawn, believable characters. —Kathleen Brachmann, Skokie Public Library, Illinois

### *Gathering Blue*
### August 2000

Gr 5-9—In Kira's community, people's cotts, or homes, are burned after an illness. After her mother dies suddenly, homeless Kira finds her former neighbors coveting the land where her cott once stood. They also resent that Kira, who was born with a deformed leg, wasn't abandoned at birth, in accordance with the society's rules. The Council of Guardians recognizes her skill at embroidery and lets her live in the Council Edifice, the one large old building left after the Ruin. Her job is to repair and restore the robe that the Singer wears during the annual Gathering that recounts the history of her community and to complete a blank section, which is to depict the future. When her young friend Matt journeys "yonder" and returns with the plants Kira needs to create blue dye and knowledge of a wider world, she pieces together the truth. The power-hungry Guardians have lied and manipulated the villagers in order to maintain their status. Kira is united with her father, whom she had believed was dead, but decides to stay at the Edifice until she embroiders a peaceful future on the robe. As in Lowry's *The Giver* (Houghton, 1993), the young protagonist is chosen by powerful adults to carry out an important task; through the exploration of this responsibility, knowledge grows, and a life-altering choice must be made. Lowry has once again created a fully realized world full of drama, suspense, and even humor. Readers won't forget these memorable characters or their struggles in an inhospitable world. —Ellen Fader, Multnomah County Library, Portland, Oregon

### *Anastasia at Your Service*
### November 1982

Gr 4-7—Fans of Anastasia will be delighted with this newest, if highly unlikely, adventure. Anastasia, now almost thirteen (and with a baby brother who, at two, is as bright as many six or maybe three-year-olds) is broke and, influenced by the Mary Roberts Rinehard Tish stories, hires herself out as, she thinks, a companion to a rich old lady. "Anastasia Atcher Service" finds herself instead treated as a scullery maid: polishing silver and serving at an elegant party where, when she dresses up to try and look older, one of her stuffed "breasts" falls into a platter of deviled eggs she's serving. To add insult to injury, one of Anastasia's school friends turns out to be her employer's granddaughter, and, to make matters worse, she hates her grandmother with a passion. How all this is resolved is slapstick, an extended joke mitigated somewhat by an almost tragic accident that happens to Anastasia's little brother and teaches Anastasia what true love really is. Kids (including reluctant junior-high readers) who like their humor broad will probably get a kick out of this and its young heroine—themselves writ larger than life. —Marjorie Lewis, Scarsdale Junior High School Library, New York

### *Anastasia Again!*
### October 1981

Gr 4-7—Two years ago, the major problem facing Anastasia Krupnik (Houghton, 1979) was the

imminent birth of a sibling. Now our intrepid heroine returns to confront a new problem. The Krupniks are moving from Cambridge, Massachusetts to the suburbs where, in Anastasia's words, everyone lives "in split-level houses with sets of matching furniture" and ladies "wear cute cotton dresses from Lord and Taylor's" and worry about ring around the collar. But despite her protests, the move is made, and Anastasia finds, as her father promised, that her preconceived notions are misconceptions. A new home, a cute boy down the street and an intriguing elderly neighbor all provide the stimulus for Anastasia's remarkable perceptions and reactions. Precocious yet prone to the exaggerations and behavior typical of early adolescence, Anastasia faces new experiences with an outrageous blend of gusto, reluctance, determination and anxiety. Lowry's prose, timing and on-target humor combine to give this protagonist credibility, and she's no less precise with secondary characters. Lowry has the ability to describe common experiences and situations in an uncommon and exuberant manner, while at the same time providing easy access for readers who will undoubtedly find that many of Anastasia's notions bear a close relation to their own.
—Marilyn Kaye, College of Librarianship, Univeristy of South Carolina, Columbia

## *Anastasia, Ask Your Analyst*
### May 1984

Gr 5-7—"How do you know I don't have symptoms of necrosis?" Anastasia, thirteen and exhibiting all the emotional signs of adolescence, is sure she needs an analyst. She's also sure that she needs gerbils, over her mother's objections. Being Anastasia, she gets both. The gerbils are ostensibly for her science project; her analyst a plaster Freud. Anastasia's sessions with Freud provide a humorous vehicle for internal monologues, and the eleven gerbils' escape provides outright comedy. As always, Lowry's dialogue captures the spirit of her subjects, and the pace is fast enough to snare most young readers. However, there is a problem with this book. Anastasia spends the bulk of the novel bemoaning the "hormones" that come with being thirteen. Conveniently, on the next-to-last page, Anastasia declares that her "hormones" are gone, along with all her other problems. It's a rare teen who recovers in a season, and we have come to expect more effective character resolution from this author. Despite this hitch, Anastasia . . . is still readable, basically credible and will be enjoyable to those who already belong to her following. —Carolyn Noah, Worcester Public Library, Massachusetts

## *Anastasia Krupnik*
## October 1979

Grades 5-7—Anastasia is ten years old. Her calm, understanding parents are about to have another child; her grandmother is mildly senile and lives in a nursing home; her teacher is kind but kind of dense. Anastasia trains most of her attention on them—and on herself. She keeps a notebook that has lists, reproduced at the end of each chapter, of "Things I Love" and "Things I Hate," and seems always to have a hand on her emotional pulse. Not only does she get stomachaches and headaches when she's upset, but even worries that she will. Granted that she is given some heavy events to absorb—birth, death, ridicule (by a boy she likes) and, especially, jealousy. Still, the focus is relentlessly on Anastasia's reactions, and, to make matters worse, the author would have us believe that a child can do her important learning through conversation with adults. Nevertheless, there are some wonderful moments which include Anastasia's complaints about her name, which is so long that if it were stencilled on a tee shirt, "the letters would go right into my armpits!" and the brief, unforgettable description of the irresistably flamboyant sixth grade boy she admires. —Mary B. Nickerson, Thayer Academy, Braintree, Massachusetts

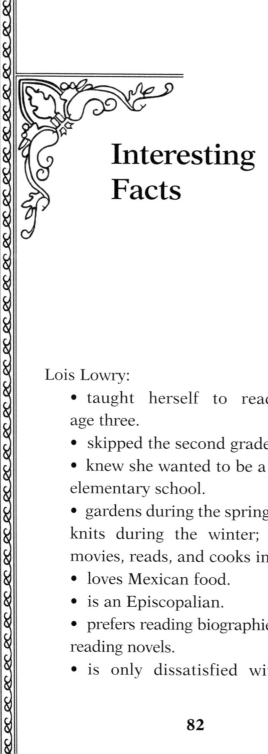

# Interesting Facts

Lois Lowry:

- taught herself to read and write at age three.
- skipped the second grade.
- knew she wanted to be a writer as early as elementary school.
- gardens during the spring and summer and knits during the winter; she goes to the movies, reads, and cooks in all seasons.
- loves Mexican food.
- is an Episcopalian.
- prefers reading biographies and memoirs to reading novels.
- is only dissatisfied with one piece of

writing she's published: the final third of *The Giver*, which she thinks is rushed because she was restricted by length—the book needed to be under 200 pages long.

• never reads children's books, even though she considers some young-adult authors—including Paula Danziger, Katherine Paterson, Phyllis Reynolds Naylor, and Jerry Spinelli—good friends.

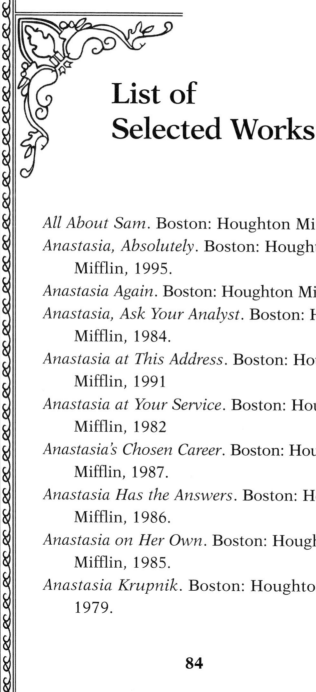

# List of
# Selected Works

*All About Sam*. Boston: Houghton Mifflin, 1988.

*Anastasia, Absolutely*. Boston: Houghton Mifflin, 1995.

*Anastasia Again*. Boston: Houghton Mifflin, 1981.

*Anastasia, Ask Your Analyst*. Boston: Houghton Mifflin, 1984.

*Anastasia at This Address*. Boston: Houghton Mifflin, 1991

*Anastasia at Your Service*. Boston: Houghton Mifflin, 1982

*Anastasia's Chosen Career*. Boston: Houghton Mifflin, 1987.

*Anastasia Has the Answers*. Boston: Houghton Mifflin, 1986.

*Anastasia on Her Own*. Boston: Houghton Mifflin, 1985.

*Anastasia Krupnik*. Boston: Houghton Mifflin, 1979.

*Attaboy, Sam!* Boston: Houghton Miffin, 1992.

*Autumn Street.* Boston: Houghton Mifflin, 1980.

*Find a Stranger, Say Goodbye.* Boston: Houghton Mifflin, 1978.

*Gathering Blue.* Boston: Houghton Mifflin, 2000.

*The Giver.* Boston: Houghton Mifflin, 1993.

*Looking Back: A Book of Memories.* Boston: Houghton Mifflin, 1998.

*Number the Stars.* Boston: Houghton Mifflin, 1989.

*The One Hundredth Thing About Caroline.* Boston: Hougthon Mifflin, 1983.

*Rabble Starkey.* Boston: Houghton Mifflin, 1987.

*See You Around, Sam!* Boston: Hougthon Mifflin, 1996.

*Stay!: Keeper's Story.* Boston: Hougthon Mifflin, 1997.

*A Summer to Die.* Boston: Houghton Mifflin, 1971.

*Switcharound.* Boston: Hougthon Mifflin, 1985.

*Taking Care of Terrific.* Boston: Hougthon Mifflin, 1983.

*Us and Uncle Fraud.* Boston: Hougthon Mifflin, 1984.

*Your Move, J. P.!* Boston: Hougthon Mifflin, 1990.

*Zooman Sam.* Boston: Hougthon Mifflin, 1999.

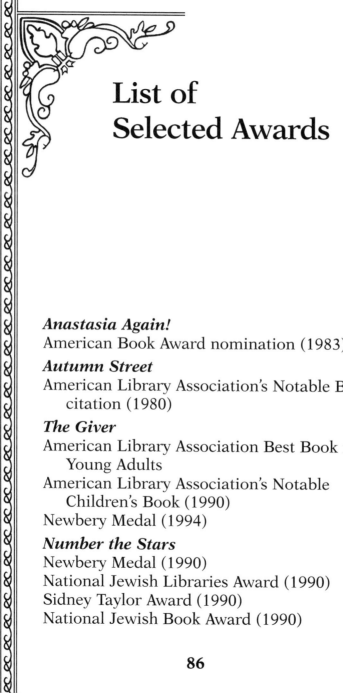

# List of
# Selected Awards

***Anastasia Again!***
American Book Award nomination (1983)

***Autumn Street***
American Library Association's Notable Book
citation (1980)

***The Giver***
American Library Association Best Book for
Young Adults
American Library Association's Notable
Children's Book (1990)
Newbery Medal (1994)

***Number the Stars***
Newbery Medal (1990)
National Jewish Libraries Award (1990)
Sidney Taylor Award (1990)
National Jewish Book Award (1990)

### Rabble Starkey

*Boston Globe/Horn Book* Award (1987)
Children's Book Committee of Bank Street
    College Award (1987)
Child Study Award (1987)
Golden Kite Award (1987)
Society of Children's Book Writers Award(1987)

### A Summer To Die

Children's Literature Award (1978)
International Reading Association Award (1978)

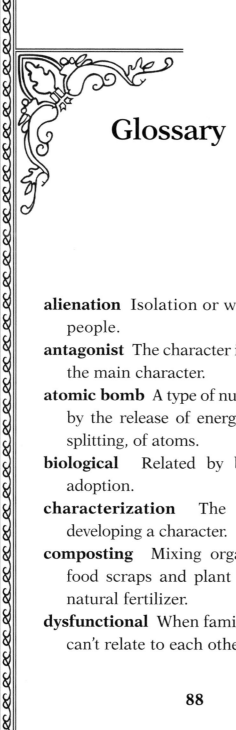

# Glossary

**alienation**  Isolation or withdrawal from other people.

**antagonist**  The character in a story who opposes the main character.

**atomic bomb**  A type of nuclear weapon powered by the release of energy from the fission, or splitting, of atoms.

**biological**  Related by birth rather than by adoption.

**characterization**  The act of creating and developing a character.

**composting**  Mixing organic matter—such as food scraps and plant clippings—for use as natural fertilizer.

**dysfunctional**  When family members or friends can't relate to each other socially.

**dystopia**  A place that seems ideal but is actually sinister. The opposite of utopia.

**editor**  A person who corrects a manuscript and advises an author before the book is published.

**enclave**  A region or community.

**extrovert**  An outgoing person who prefers to be around other people much of the time.

**fiction**  A story that is not based on fact or actual events.

**flashback**  The interruption of a past event into a story.

**foreshadowing**  A suggestion of what is to come in a story.

**Hiroshima**  A city in southwestern Japan. The United States dropped the first atomic bomb ever used against an enemy on Hiroshima on August 6, 1945, killing more than 60,000 people and destroying four square miles (ten square kilometers) of the city.

**historical fiction**  Stories where make-believe characters experience real-life events.

***Horn Book Magazine***  A bimonthly journal offering book reviews and articles about children's literature.

**innuendo**  A subtle insinuation or hint.

**introvert**  A shy person who prefers to be alone much of the time.

**Nagasaki**  A city in western Japan. The U.S.

dropped the second atomic bomb ever used against an enemy over Nagasaki on August 9, 1945, three days after bombing Hiroshima. One-third of the city was destroyed and 40,000 people were killed

**narrative**  The way a story is told.

**nonfiction**  A written account of actual events.

**novelist**  A person who writes full-length fiction books.

**objective**  Based on facts, and not influenced by opinion or bias.

**occult**  Relating to the supernatural or magic.

**paleontologist**  A scientist who studies fossils to learn about prehistoric life.

**plot**  The events that take place over the course of a story or novel.

**protagonist**  The main character in a story.

*Publisher's Weekly*  A highly respected news magazine about all aspects of the publishing industry.

*School Library Journal*  A magazine geared toward librarians who work with young people and children's literature.

**setting**  Where and when a story takes place.

**sophisticated**  Complicated and experienced.

**subjective**  Based on opinion or bias, not on facts.

**subtext**  A second layer of meaning in a story.

**theme** A recurring idea in a story.

**tributary** A body of water that flows into a larger body of water, such as a river into a lake or sea.

**utopia** An ideal place.

**voice** The style and tone of a story.

# For More Information

## Web Sites

Due to the changing nature of Internet links, the Rosen Publishing Group, Inc., has developed an online list of Web sites related to the subject of this book. This site is updated regularly. Please use this link to access the list:

http://www.rosenlinks.com/lab/llow/

# For Further Reading

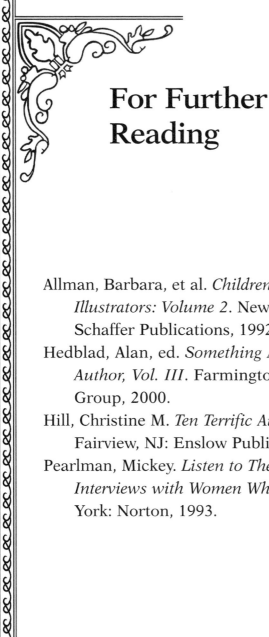

Allman, Barbara, et al. *Children's Authors and Illustrators: Volume 2*. New York: Frank Schaffer Publications, 1992.

Hedblad, Alan, ed. *Something About the Author, Vol. III*. Farmington Hills, MI: Gale Group, 2000.

Hill, Christine M. *Ten Terrific Authors for Teens*. Fairview, NJ: Enslow Publishers, 2000.

Pearlman, Mickey. *Listen to Their Voice: Twenty Interviews with Women Who Write*. New York: Norton, 1993.

# Bibliography

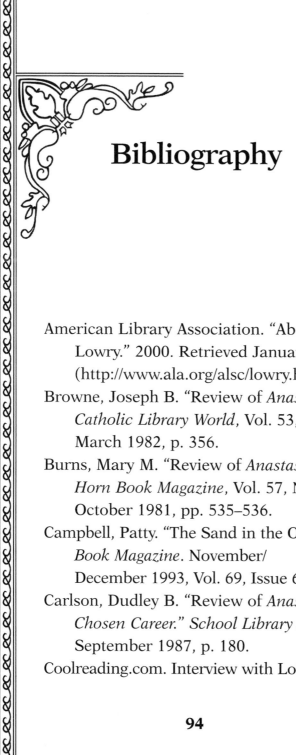

American Library Association. "About Lois Lowry." 2000. Retrieved January 2002 (http://www.ala.org/alsc/lowry.html).

Browne, Joseph B. "Review of *Anastasia Again!*" *Catholic Library World*, Vol. 53, No. 8, March 1982, p. 356.

Burns, Mary M. "Review of *Anastasia Again!*" *Horn Book Magazine*, Vol. 57, No. 5, October 1981, pp. 535–536.

Campbell, Patty. "The Sand in the Oyster." *Horn Book Magazine*. November/ December 1993, Vol. 69, Issue 6, p. 717.

Carlson, Dudley B. "Review of *Anastasia's Chosen Career.*" *School Library Journal*, September 1987, p. 180.

Coolreading.com. Interview with Lois Lowry.

Retrieved December 2001 (http://www.coolreading.com/alda.php3/studio/ questions/ilois).

Cooper, Ilene. "Review of *Your Move, J. P.!*" *Booklist*, March 1, 1990, p. 1345.

Currier, Tammy. "Author Profile: Lois Lowry." Teenreads.com. 2000. Retrieved December 2001 (http://teenreads.com/authors/ au-lowry-lois.asp).

Elleman, Barbara. "Review of *Autumn Street.*" *Booklist*, Vol. 76, No. 16, April 15, 1980, p. 1206.

Gale Group. Contemporary Authors Online database. Farmington Hills, MI: The Gale Group, 1999.

Hedblad, Alan, ed. *Something About the Author, Vol. III*. Farmington Hills, MI: Gale Group, Inc., 2000. pp. 122–128.

Hobbs, Mary. "Review of *A Summer to Die.*" *The Junior Bookshelf*, Vol. 43, No. 4, August 1979, pp. 224–225.

Hurst, Carol Otis. "Other Worlds, Our World." *Teaching Pre-K*, Vol. 31, Issue 4, January 2001, p. 74.

Hurst, Carol. "Featured Author: Lois Lowry." 1999. Retrieved November 2001 (http://carolhurst.com/authors/llowry.html).

Kaye, Marilyn. "Review of *Anastasia Again!*" *School Library Journal*, Vol. 28, No. 2, October 1981, p. 144.

Koch, John. "The Interview: Lois Lowry." *Boston Globe Magazine*, December 20, 1998. Retrieved December 2001 (http://www.boston.com/globe/magazine/12-20/interview.shtml).

Lodge, Sally. "Lois Lowry: Snapshots from Her Life." *Publishers Weekly*, Vol. 245, No. 36, September 7, 1998, p. 29.

Lorraine, Walter. "Lois Lowry." *Horn Book Magazine*, Vol. 70, Issue 4, July/August 1994, p. 423.

Lowry, Lois. "Ask the Author: Legendary Author Lois Lowry." Write4Kids.com. Retrieved December 2001 (http://www.write4kids.com/answer2.html).

Lowry, Lois. "A Message From the Author." Retrieved January 2002 (http://www.randomhouse.com/teachers.guides/give.html).

Lowry, Lois. "Autobiographical Sketch Written for the Fifth Book of Junior Authors & Illustrators, 1983." Reprinted by the Educational Paperback Association. Retrieved November 2001 (http://www.edupaperback.org/authorbios/Lowry_Lois.html).

Lowry, Lois. "Lois Lowry." Contributed to the Internet Public Library by Houghton Mifflin Company. 1996. Retrieved December 2002 (http://www.ipl.org/youth/AskAuthor/Lowry.html).

Lowry, Lois. "Newbery Medal Acceptance." *Horn

*Book Magazine*, July/August 1990, Vol. 66, Issue 4, p. 412.

Lowry, Lois. "Newbery Medal Acceptance," *Horn Book Magazine*, July/August 1994, Vol. 74, Issue 4, p. 414.

Lowry, Lois. *A Summer to Die*. New York: Bantam Books, 1979.

Lowry, Lois. *Looking Back: A Book of Memories*. Boston: Houghton Mifflin, 1998.

Lowry, Lois. *The Giver*. Boston: Houghton Mifflin, 1993.

Random House Online. "Lois Lowry." 1999. Retrieved December 2001 (http://www.randomhouse.com/teachers/ authors/lowr.html).

Scholastic Press. "Lois Lowry Interview Transcript." 2001. Retrieved January 2002 (http://teacher.scholastic.com/ authorsandbooks/authors/lowry/tscript.htm).

Silver, Linda R. "Review of *A Summer to Die*." *School Library Journal*, May 1977, pp. 62–63.

Singer, Marilyn R. "Review of *Autumn Street*." *School Library Journal*, Vol. 26, No. 8, April 1980, pp. 125–126.

Sutton, Roger. "*Gathering Blue* (Book Review)." *Horn Book Magazine*, Vol. 76, Issue 5, September/October 2000, p. 573.

Twitchell, Ethel R. "Review of *Your Move, J. P.*"

*Horn Book Magazine*. March–April 1990, pp. 201–202.

Walter, Virginia A. "Lecture by Children's Author Lois Lowry Keeps Frances Clarke Sayers' Memory Alive." News for UCLA's Graduate School of Education & Information Studies, Vol. 1, No. 3, Summer 1997.

Zaidman, Laura M. "Lois Lowry." *Dictionary of Literary Biography*, Vol. 52. Farmington Hills, MI: The Gale Group, Inc., 1986.

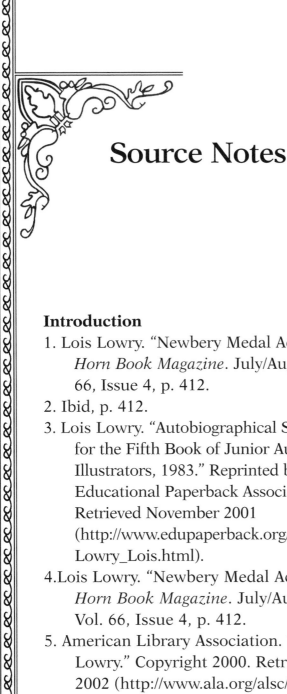

# Source Notes

## Introduction

1. Lois Lowry. "Newbery Medal Acceptance." *Horn Book Magazine*. July/August 1990, Vol. 66, Issue 4, p. 412.
2. Ibid, p. 412.
3. Lois Lowry. "Autobiographical Sketch Written for the Fifth Book of Junior Authors & Illustrators, 1983." Reprinted by the Educational Paperback Association. Retrieved November 2001 (http://www.edupaperback.org/authorbios/Lowry_Lois.html).
4. Lois Lowry. "Newbery Medal Acceptance." *Horn Book Magazine*. July/August 1990, Vol. 66, Issue 4, p. 412.
5. American Library Association. "About Lois Lowry." Copyright 2000. Retrieved January 2002 (http://www.ala.org/alsc/lowry.html).

6. Joseph B. Browne. "Review of *Anastasia Again!*" *Catholic Library World*, Vol. 52, No. 8, March 1982, p. 356.
7. Random House Online. "Lois Lowry." 1999. Retrieved December 2001 (http://www.randomhouse.com/teachers/authors/lowr.html).
8. Contemporary Authors Online database. Farmington Hills, MI: The Gale Group, 1999.

**Chapter 1**
1. Coolreading.com. "Interview with Lois Lowry." Retrieved December 2001. (http://www.coolreading.com/alda.php3/studio/questions/ilois).
2. Alan Hedblad, ed. *Something About the Author*, Vol. 111. Farmington Hills, MI: Gale Group, 2000, pp. 122–128.
3. Scholastic Press. "Lois Lowry Interview Transcript." 2001. Retrieved January 2002 (http://teacher.scholastic.com/authorsandbooks/authors/lowry/tscript.htm).
4. Tammy Currier. "Author Profile: Lois Lowry." Teenreads.com. 2000. Retrieved December 2001 (http://teenreads.com/authors/au-lowry-lois.asp).
5. Lois Lowry. "Lois Lowry." Contributed to the Internet Public Library by Houghton Mifflin Company. 1996. Retrieved December 2002

(http://www.ipl.org/youth/AskAuthor/
Lowry.html).

6. Scholastic Press. "Lois Lowry Interview Transcript." Copyright 2001. Retrieved January 2002 (http://teacher.scholastic.com/ authorsandbooks/authors/lowry/tscript.htm).

7. Lois Lowry. "Lois Lowry." Contributed to the Internet Public Library by Houghton Mifflin Company. 1996. Retrieved December 2002 (http://www.ipl.org/youth/AskAuthor/Lowry.html).

8. Lois Lowry. *Looking Back: A Book of Memories.* Boston, MA: Houghton Mifflin, 1998.

9. Virginia A. Walter "Lecture by Children's Author Lois Lowry Keeps Frances Clarke Sayers' Memory Alive." News for UCLA's Graduate School of Education & Information Studies, Vol. 1, No. 3, Summer 1997.

10. Sally Lodge. "Lois Lowry: Snapshots From Her Life." *Publishers Weekly,* Vol. 245, No. 36, September 7, 1998, p. 29.

11. Alan Hedblad, ed. *Something About the Author,* Vol. 111. Farmington Hills, Michigan, Gale Group, 2000, pp. 122–128

12. Lois Lowry. "Lois Lowry." Contributed to the Internet Public Library by Houghton Mifflin Company. 1996. Retrieved December 2002 (http://www.ipl.org/youth/AskAuthor/Lowry.html).

13. Scholastic Press. "Lois Lowry Interview Transcript." 2001. Retrieved January 2002

(http://teacher.scholastic.com/authorsandbooks/ authors/lowry/tscript.htm).

14. Walter Lorraine. "Lois Lowry." *Horn Book Magazine*, Vol. 70, Issue 4, July/August 1994, p. 423.

**Chapter 2**

1. Lois Lowry. "Newbery Medal Acceptance." *Horn Book Magazine*, July/August 1994, Vol. 74, Issue 4, p. 414.

2. Lois Lowry. "Lois Lowry." Contributed to the Internet Public Library by Houghton Mifflin Company. 1996. Retrieved December 2002 (http://www.ipl.org/youth/AskAuthor/Lowry.html).

3. John Koch. "The Interview: Lois Lowry." *Boston Globe Magazine*. December 20, 1998. Retrieved December 2001 (http://www.boston.com/globe/ magazine/12-20/interview.shtml).

4. Lois Lowry. "Ask the Author: Legendary Author Lois Lowry." Write4Kids.com. Retrieved December 2001 (http://www.write4kids.com/ answer2.html).

5. Coolreading.com. Interview. Retrieved December 2001. (http://www.coolreading.com/alda.php3/ studio/questions/ilois).

6. Scholastic Press. "Lois Lowry Interview Transcript." Interview with students. 2001. Retrieved January 2002 (http://teacher.scholastic.com/authorsandbooks/ authors/lowry/tscript.htm).

7. Ibid.
8. Coolreading.com. Interview. Retrieved December 2001. (http://www.coolreading.com/ alda.php3/studio/questions/ilois).
9. John Koch. "The Interview: Lois Lowry." *Boston Globe Magazine*. December 20, 1998. Retrieved December 2001 (http://www.boston.com/globe/ magazine/12–20/interview.shtml).
10. Random House Online. "Lois Lowry." 1999. Retrieved December 2001 (http://www.randomhouse.com/teachers/ authors/lowr.html).
11. Scholastic Press. "Lois Lowry Interview Transcript." 2001. Retrieved January 2002 (http://teacher.scholastic.com/authorsandbooks/ authors/lowry/tscript.htm).
12. John Koch. "The Interview: Lois Lowry." *Boston Globe Magazine*. December 20, 1998. Retrieved December 2001 (http://www.boston.com/ globe/magazine/12–20/interview.shtml).
13. Lois Lowry. "Ask the Author: Legendary Author Lois Lowry." Write4Kids.com. Retrieved December 2001 (http://www.write4kids.com/ answer2.html).
14. John Koch. "The Interview: Lois Lowry." *Boston Globe Magazine*. December 20, 1998. Retrieved December 2001 (http://www.boston.com/globe/magazine/ 12-20/interview.shtml).

## Chapter 3

1. Sally Lodge. "Lois Lowry: Snapshots From Her Life." *Publishers Weekly*, Vol. 245, No. 36, September 7, 1998, p. 29.
2. John Koch. "The Interview: Lois Lowry." *Boston Globe Magazine*. December 20, 1998. Retrieved December 2001 (http://www.boston.com/ globe/magazine/12-20/interview.shtml).
3. Sally Lodge. "Lois Lowry: Snapshots from Her Life." *Publishers Weekly*, Vol. 245, No. 36, Sept. 7, 1998, p. 29.
4. Ibid.
5. Alan Hedblad, ed. *Something About the Author*, Vol. 111. Farmington Hills, MI: Gale Group, Inc., 2000, pp. 122–128.
6. Lois Lowry. "Newbery Medal Acceptance." *Horn Book Magazine*. July/August 1994, Vol. 74, Issue 4, p. 414.
7. Lois Lowry. *Looking Back: A Book of Memories*. Boston: Houghton-Mifflin, 1998.

## Chapter 4

1. Campbell, Patty. "The Sand in the Oyster." *Horn Book Magazine*, November/December 1993, Vol. 69, Issue 6, p. 717.
2. Sally Lodge. "Lois Lowry: Snapshots from Her Life." *Publishers Weekly*, Vol. 245, No. 36, September 7, 1998, p. 29.
3. Lois Lowry. *A Summer to Die*. New York: Bantam Books, 1979.

4. Mary Hobbs. "Review of *A Summer to Die*." *The Junior Bookshelf*, Vol. 43, No. 4, August 1979, pp. 224–225.
5. Marilyn R. Singer. "Review of *Autumn Street*." *School Library Journal*, Vol. 26, No. 8, April 1980, pp. 125–126.
6. Random House Online. "Lois Lowry." 1999. Retrieved December 2001 (http://www.randomhouse.com/teachers/ authors/lowr.html).
7. Barbara Elleman. "Review of *Autumn Street*." *Booklist*, Vol. 76, No. 16, April 15, 1980, p. 1206.
8. Mary M. Burns. "Review of *Anastasia Again!*" *Horn Book Magazine*, Vol. 57, No. 5, October 1981, pp. 535–536.
9. Marilyn Kaye. "Review of *Anastasia Again!*" *School Library Journal*, Vol. 28, No. 2, October 1981, p. 144.
10. Dudley B. Carlson. "Review of *Anastasia's Chosen Career*." *School Library Journal*, September 1987, p. 180.
11. Ethel R. Twitchell. "Review of *Your Move, J. P.!*" *Horn Book Magazine*, March/April 1990, pp. 201–202.
12. Ilene Cooper. "Review of *Your Move, J. P.!*" *Booklist*, March 1, 1990, p.1345.
13. Tammy Currier. "Author Profile: Lois Lowry." Teenreads.com. 2000. Retrieved December 2001 (http://teenreads.com/authors/ au-lowry-lois.asp).

14. Patty Campbell. "The Sand in the Oyster." *Horn Book Magazine*, November/December 1993, Vol. 69, Issue 6, p. 717

15. Carol Otis Hurst. "Other Worlds, Our World." *Teaching Pre-K*, Vol. 31, Issue 4, Jan. 2001, p. 74.

16. Roger Sutton. "*Gathering Blue* (Book Review)." *Horn Book Magazine*, Vol. 76, Issue 5, September/October 2000, p. 573.

17. Random House Online. "Lois Lowry." 1999. Retrieved December 2001 (http://www.randomhouse.com/teachers/authors/lowr.html).

18. Scholastic Press. "Lois Lowry Interview Transcript." 2001. Retrieved January 2002 (http://teacher.scholastic.com/authorsandbooks/authors/lowry/tscript.htm).

19. John Koch. "The Interview: Lois Lowry." *Boston Globe Magazine*. December 20, 1998. Retrieved December 2001 (http://www.boston.com/globe/magazine/12-20/interview.shtml).

20. Scholastic Press. "Lois Lowry Interview Transcript." 2001. Retrieved January 2002 (http://teacher.scholastic.com/authorsandbooks/authors/lowry/tscript.htm).

21. Lois Lowry. "Newbery Medal Acceptance." *Horn Book Magazine*, July/August 1994, Vol. 74, Issue 4, p. 414.

22. Scholastic Press. "Lois Lowry Interview Transcript." 2001. Retrieved January 2002

(http://teacher. scholastic.com/
authorsandbooks/authors/lowry/tscript.htm).

## Chapter 5

1. Lois Lowry. "Ask the Author: Legendary Author
Lois Lowry." Write4Kids.com. Retrieved
December 2001
(http://www.write4kids.com/answer2.html).
2. Walter Lorraine. "Lois Lowry." *Horn Book
Magazine*, Vol. 70, Issue 4, July/August 1994,
p. 423.
3. Lois Lowry. "Newbery Medal Acceptance." *Horn
Book Magazine*, July/August 1990, Vol. 66,
Issue 4, p. 412.
4. Lois Lowry. "Lois Lowry." Contributed to the
Internet Public Library by Houghton Mifflin
Company. 1996. Retrieved December 2002
(http://www.ipl.org/youth/AskAuthor/
Lowry.html).
5. Scholastic Press. "Lois Lowry Interview
Transcript." 2001. Retrieved January 2002
(http://teacher.scholastic.com/authorsandbooks/
authors/lowry/tscript.htm).
6. Lois Lowry. "Lois Lowry." Contributed to the
Internet Public Library by Houghton Mifflin
Company. 1996. Retrieved December 2002
(http://www.ipl.org/youth/AskAuthor/Lowry.html).
7. John Koch. "The Interview: Lois Lowry." *Boston
Globe Magazine*. December 20, 1998. Retrieved

December 2001 (http://www.boston.com/globe/
magazine/12-20/interview.shtml).
8. Lois Lowry. "Newbery Medal Acceptance." *Horn
Book Magazine*. July/August 1990, Vol. 66, Issue
4, p. 412.

# Index

# G

*Gathering Blue*, 49–50, 51
Germany, 16, 31, 39
*Giver, The*, 9, 20, 22, 34, 49,
   51, 52, 53–56

# H

Harry Potter books, 53
Harvard University, 18, 19
Hawaii, 14, 40
Hiroshima, 16
Holocaust, 16
*Horn Book Magazine*, 20, 43,
   45–46, 49, 50, 51, 52, 58
Houghton Mifflin, 20

# I

*I Know Why the Caged Bird
   Sings*, 53
*Indian Captive: The Story of
   Mary Jemison*, 18

# J

Japan, 15–16, 26, 34–37

# L

Lenski, Lois, 18
*Looking Back: A Book of
   Memories*, 17, 31, 32,
   33, 40
Lorraine, Walter, 20, 58
Lowry, Donald (husband), 9,
   18, 19
Lowry, Grey (son), 19, 31–32
Lowry, Lois
   adolescence of, 17

autobiography of, 17, 31,
   32, 33, 40
Anastasia Krupnik books
   by, 8, 11–12, 13, 17, 19,
   22, 28, 44–47, 48, 53
   awards of, 7, 8, 9, 10
   books by, 8, 9 17, 20, 22,
   26, 27, 28, 31, 32, 33,
   34, 40, 42–56
   characters of, 10–11, 13,
   28, 29, 53
   childhood of, 12, 13, 14–16,
   17–18, 23, 33, 34–37
   children of, 9, 19, 23, 31
   and college, 18, 19, 37–38
   and controversy, 53–56
   daily life of, 19, 29–30
   and death of son, 31–32
   dystopic novels of, 49–52
   early career of, 9–10
   early favorite books of,
   17–18
   editor for, 20, 58
   facts about, 82–83
   on fiction vs. nonfiction,
   25–26
   grandchildren of, 32
   hobbies of, 19
   home of, 19, 20–21
   husband of, 9, 18, 19
   inspiration for books of,
   23–24, 25, 32–41
   interview with, 63–69
   on Japan, 15–16, 34–37
   maiden name of, 14
   and the Newbery Medal, 7,

# About the Author

Susanna Daniel is a freelance writer and poet living in Wisconsin. Her fiction has been anthologized and published in literary magazines, and she has taught creative writing and literature at the Universities of Iowa and Wisconsin.

# Photo Credits

Cover, p. 2 courtesy of Lois Lowry.

# Series Design and Layout

Tahara Hasan

# Editor

Annie Sommers